beyond survival

Hazelden titles of related interest

Daybreak: Meditations for Women Survivors of Sexual Abuse by Maureen Brady

The Healing Way: Adult Recovery from Childhood Sexual Abuse by Kristin A. Kunzman

beyond survival

*a writing journey for
healing childhood sexual abuse*

Maureen Brady

A Hazelden Book
HarperCollins*Publishers*

FIRST HARPERCOLLINS EDITION PUBLISHED IN 1992

ISBN 0–06–255294–5
LC 91–59056

92   93   94   95   96   **MAL**   10   9   8   7   6   5   4   3   2   1

This edition is printed on acid-free paper that meets the American National
Standards Institute Z39.48 Standard.

This book is dedicated to *the healing* from childhood sexual abuse—yours, mine, and that of our society. Each time we hear our story, whether we tell it or listen to another survivor tell it, there is a contribution made to the healing.

I would like to thank the following people for their support during the conception and writing of this book: Jackie Harding, Marilyn Hauser, Suzannah Lessard, Stephen Roos, Belles Sanborn, Vivian Ubell, and my editor, Pat Boland. For contributing samples of the writing exercises, I am deeply grateful to Danielle, Diane, Elvia, Kenny, Mike, Richard, and Tsurah.

contents

beyond survival

introduction

We cannot live without our lives.
—Barbara Deming

about healing

Welcome to this journey beyond survival. Everyone who has been the victim of childhood sexual abuse and lived to tell his or her story is a survivor. There are far too many of us. We are women and men. We come from all races and all classes. We live in every state and region, every country. Many of us have honed our survival skills to the bone, and, rightly, we are proud of this. We are making it. We have pulled through against great odds without capsizing. But we deserve much more.

I remember a day early in my relationship with a new therapist. I was reporting all of the childhood sexual abuse that I had dug up and ploughed through when she stopped me to ask, "And what have you done so far to heal from this?" I was stunned and said nothing. What came vividly into my mind's eye was a picture of how raw my wounds still were. I realized I had little vision of the possibilities for that ever changing. From that day on, I've concentrated a lot more on healing.

When we cut our finger, we witness what happens in the wound healing. We bring the sides of a cut together, then cover and protect it until the tissue repairs itself. We see that it heals, though it leaves a scar. Our incest wounds, too, can heal with scarring. The scar will never be the same as the original skin of the finger, but it will be healed nonetheless. Scar tissue has some remarkable qualities. It is tough and not very pliant in the beginning. Then it softens remarkably with time. So, too, does our psychic scar.

One reason it has been difficult for us to bring our stories up from the underground into the light of day is that until quite recently, there were so very few stories written down for us to see. We are taught that incest is taboo when what seems closer to the truth is that *disclosing* the incest is taboo. As the testimonials of more and more pioneering survivors are recorded, they show us the value of our efforts to give voice to ourselves. We see in them the worth of encountering the pain of remembering. These stories become pillars in a foundation of a new truth—*our truth.*

Realizing how deeply empowering it is to read the stories of others, we can visualize the potency of all of our stories being recorded. Whether we put them away for private safekeeping, ritually burn them, or share them with others, each one of us who records our story provides another pillar. Your story will add to that foundation.

The weekly topics in this book have been arranged in a sequence that approximates the progress of many survivors in their healing. Keep in mind that we each follow our own path, that we all have leaps as well as stalls and even times when we feel as if we were going backward. While my primary concern has been to provide tools for survivors of sexual abuse, survivors of other types of abuse—physical, emotional, or, as one friend put it, anyone recovering from childhood—will also find this book helpful and validating.

the writing exercises

You are a human being who has been given words as one means of communication, probably the most exact and direct one, even if it is not the mode closest to your nature. As someone who was abused in childhood, sexually or otherwise, you were forced to silence your side of the story. My simple belief is this: *to heal, you need to tell it.* If you are a writer, fine. If you are not a writer, fine. Each of us has the ability to write things down and change from having done that. That is why I've included a writing exercise with each topic.

There are times when words do not work. Some of our experiences are preverbal. If you want to draw a picture in response to a writing exercise, please do. If you want to get up and move your body in a particular way to express yourself, if you want to growl and snarl at someone in the mirror, please do. It's your journey, and "being good," following all the rules, is not the route to freedom. But it is my hope that you will take the pencil to paper most of the time. And when you reach the last page and look back to see what you have written, you will find that you have recorded the essence of your story.

There are fifty-two topics so that you can conveniently use this book for a weekly exercise on your journey. You might want to join a weekly group so you can use it with others, either doing the reading and writing separately and then gathering to share and discuss your responses, or even doing the reading and writing together. Some of you will prefer to do it on your own and on your own schedule. Choose the way that is right for you. Remember to be gentle. That is always the way to healing.

Most of the writing exercises are designed to launch you into a free-wheeling storytelling that will move you into a piece of your story or a particular angle on it. Some abuse survivors have shared their stories in response to the first ten exercises—these stories begin on page 166. Look to these to help free yourself if you're stuck. I suggest you write for twenty minutes for each exercise. You can, of course, always go on longer or continue later on with something you started. But let it be freeing to you to know you are only going to write for twenty minutes. Set a timer, if you like, or write your starting time at the beginning of the exercise. Don't censor yourself or spend half of the time throwing out the first, second, or third impulse that comes to you. Trust that what comes first is what wants to be recorded, and go for it. If you have a judge who sits on your shoulder saying, "This is too trivial," or "This is not relevant," tell the judge that this journey is not for him or her. Leave this character behind now. If you have a tendency to hoard, to save up your thoughts or pieces of your story for later, try leaving that behind also. When we hoard, we block the flow. When we use what is given now, the well fills anew.

the vision and action

It is difficult to move out of the strictures of the past unless we have a vision of what we are moving on to. If we see freedom only as a vast space ahead of us, as unbounded as the horizon on the Great Plains, we are likely to be as lost as we were in victimhood, where we were at least able to define ourselves by the walls all around us. This is why it is helpful to permit ourselves a visualization every week, or as often as we want to.

Your visualization can be as broad or as specific as you want it to be. I suggest you try from the very first week to write down your vision, but in case you have trouble getting started, there are examples included for the first dozen topics. You are welcome to borrow those visions or elaborate on them or just bounce off them. Besides writing it in your book, you might want to write your vision on a scrap of paper and put it in a place in your home where you can't lose sight of it for long—the bathroom mirror, next to where you eat, or by your bedside. Visualization is enriching. It means welcoming the gift of your imagination to take an active part in the unfolding of your destiny. As incest survivors we may feel, *Do not touch; this is for others whose lives were not screwed up like ours, not for us.* But I urge you to try it. Visualizations are for everyone.

We can also take action, and when we do, we find it healing. Use the weekly action to bring yourself to the moment, to realize the places where you tend toward paralysis. The choice to take small steps is often what brings us back into the flow of life. Through simple actions we flex our muscles and realize our strength. Over time, without denying what we have come through, we build ourselves anew.

I wish you a heartening and healing journey.

Remembering

The body's memory has integrity. It has stored both our experience and our unfelt feelings. Some of us spent many years in a state of amnesia about our incest, yet once we make the first admission, we realize it is more accurate to look back on the "amnesia" as a state of "pre-knowing" than "not-knowing." Because our bodies did know. Denial protected us, whether from the facts or the feelings. It protects us still from releasing more than we can handle at once. Yet inside, on some deeper plane, we know the whole story.

To live with balance we need to stand on the firm foundation of our experience. But isn't it awfully shaky to stand on the shattering occurrences we suffered in which we were invaded, overrun, and deeply wounded? Would we not do better to leave it forgotten and go on building above ground?

Many of us have admirably built above ground, developing our careers and talents, raising our children, being active citizens in the world. Yet no matter how good we looked on the outside, the cost was that often, on the inside, we did not feel whole. We've remained connected in a ghostly relationship to the past, being either repeatedly drawn to re-create it in the present, or filled with longing for what was not satisfied.

Parts of us have been split off, psychologically amputated, leaving us feeling fragmented. For instance, perhaps our anger travels along parallel to us as if it were in a sidecar but does not get expressed as part of us. Some of us have developed multiple personalities. Some of us have needed to function with a persona, such as the worker, the performer, the athlete, or the seductress, to be comfortable. What does it mean to re-member ourselves? At this time in our lives we deserve to sit still, call in all our parts and embody them, so that we can hold ourselves, lovingly remembered.

Let us trust that we each know where to begin. We have everything we need in storage and most of it can stay there. We do not need to barter over which memory is most important, nor do we need to try to get out everything at once.

writing exercise:

Right now the uppermost memory that comes to me is when . . . (Add on to this sentence and continue writing for twenty minutes.)

vision:

Think about and write a vision for yourself for the week. You might want it to be a vision that relates to memory. For example, my vision is to remember the whole picture of what it was like to be me at age eight.

action:

Write about an action you would like to practice daily or take some time for during the next week. Again, try to make it an action that relates to remembering. For example, my action is to look myself in the eye in the mirror every day and say, "What you remember is true. It really happened, and it happened to you."

Breaking the silence

Most of us who were sexually abused as children were forced to swallow our feelings, to silence them rather than express them. Given that we were dependent on the very people who abused us, this was essential for our survival. We may have made stabs at telling, only to find ourselves threatened. Often the threats contained charges—"If you tell, I'll get you," "I'll say you asked for it," "You'll be hurt worse than you can imagine"—that turned us back in on ourselves and provoked shame.

In trying to build our lives in spite of and around this silence, we experienced short-lived moments of freedom, but quite soon bumped again into the constraints of our armor. Keeping the silence is consuming and pervasive. Someone offends us, but we are not able to say so. Our world narrows a little. Our feeling is swallowed. Deep in our gut we are holding tension to keep it all down. We are paying the price for what someone else did to us. Keeping the silence has hurt us for a long while.

Breaking the silence is an act of courage that can lead to our healing. It is important to choose someone trustworthy to share with—a therapist, a friend, a group of recovering incest survivors—someone who will believe us unconditionally. Often before we can do this, we must break a silence we have kept within ourselves. To do this in writing can be a way to capture our experience, to reel it in from where it has resided in the ocean of our unconscious life.

Once we have done this, we may feel greatly relieved. Or we may discover ourselves in a wilderness fraught with fear for our newly exposed self. Or we may feel both of these feelings simultaneously. We are rearranging our underpinnings. The change may be overwhelming at first.

Breaking the silence is not a one-time event. We break it to ourselves; then we go on to tell another. Some of us eventually open up the subject with our perpetrator. Some of us speak out publicly. At every juncture where we tell, we go back through a process. We come to know this process like a road map. Yet we forget—especially when our feelings tell us disaster is befalling us in our new, tender skin—that we are on a journey and not stuck in a tunnel with no light to guide us. Besides our familiarity with clutching at silence, we are also developing a familiarity with walking toward a new freedom.

writing exercise:

I could not tell . . . (Complete the following sentence and go on writing for twenty minutes.)

vision:

(Example: My vision is for freedom from secrets.)

action:

(Example: My action is to tell someone all I know about some piece of my story, including the feelings I am aware of.)

Cracking denial

Denial protected us, screening out certain experiences and feelings until we grew strong enough to relate to them. We might not have survived without denial. Yet it also dropped a curtain over our experience, obscuring it, leaving us with a sense of missing pieces. For instance, when we achieved something, we felt like an imposter. Or, though we had a relationship with a significant other, we often felt alone and unrelated to anyone.

Many of us remembered the abusive acts or scenarios, but our denial buffered us against believing that these acts had a significant effect on us. "So what, it only happened a few times," we said, or "What good will it do me to focus on it when it's done and can never be undone?"

Some of us didn't remember the incest at all but were plagued by unexplained symptoms, such as fear of the dark, self-abusive or self-mutilating behaviors (ranging from chronically putting ourselves down to literally pulling our hair out), or having an inordinately hard time saying no. While we felt extremely powerless over these fears or reactions, we could not begin to make sense of them until we cracked our denial and began to remember more about the abuse we had suffered.

A cracked surface under pressure opens wider and wider. When we break through our denial, we fear a fall into a deep abyss. While it is true we may encounter great fear, anxiety, and pain, our denial does not fall away all at once. We only see as much as we can bear to see at any given time. The rest is saved for later. Further, we can actively say, "This is enough for me now. I must stop and rest and integrate what I see before I can move forward."

Despite whatever we intellectually know about denial, when we come out of it we are likely to be thrown off balance and suddenly see every human interaction through a lens of incest. We have little trust. We may feel as if incest were lurking around every corner, and we may lose a sense of how any touch could be good touch. These feelings pass with the perspective of time as we continue our healing. For now we need to look at the particular place where our denial has been lifted.

writing exercise:

I used to think _____ (Fill in with something as specific as *my uncle made me sit on his lap in a weird way,* or as broad as *the incest happened but didn't mean anything.* The latter isn't true; it did mean something. *It meant . . .* Write for twenty minutes about what it meant then and what it has meant throughout your life until now.)

vision:

(Example: I visualize new roots growing out of my truth.)

action:

(Example: I will remind myself every day this week that I have been deeply affected by the abuse. I will remind myself also that admitting the truth of that is a first step toward healing.)

Assessing the damages

Where we had blocked off recognition, we are now looking to see what we were avoiding. It will be hard not to swing entirely from avoidance to the other end of the pendulum, where we are extremely sensitive to and overwhelmed by the acuteness of our wounds. We may feel deeply shattered. Perhaps it feels as if we are bleeding to death inside and have no way to stop the flow now that it has started. It is hard to reconcile the idea that we can be *this injured* and yet have lived as if this part of us did not exist until quite recently. To get some balance, we must do the job of assessing our damages. It is wise to have some help with this from a therapist as well as from other survivors, and to recognize that the sooner we can make an assessment, the better. We need to find freedom from that feeling that we *are* this damage.

Our woundedness, which we had struggled so hard to camouflage or ignore, now may demand enormous amounts of our energy. We find ourselves hard put to function, to do simple tasks that we once took for granted, such as crossing the street on a green light, instead of on a red, or getting to work on time. We feel very tender and highly sensitive in our interactions with others. We are likely to be needy, and, to confound us further, we are ashamed of being needy.

We can seek balance by writing down two or three incidents of abuse and documenting our sense—now—of the effects these had on us. Once we have recorded this much of the past, we will be more free to rest without the fear that we are re-entering denial or using other old defenses.

writing exercise:

I don't need to list all of my damages, but the ones I want to write about at this moment are . . .

vision:
(Example: I will close my eyes and see myself as I was as a child, walking toward me. In what way do I look wounded? How do I feel about it?)

action:
(Example: I will ask this child-part of myself what I can do for her or him. I will do my best to follow through and do it.)

Recognizing powerlessness

Despite our efforts to write things down, share them with others, and use every tool at our disposal to keep track of what we are discovering about incest, we are still very likely to be overwhelmed with feelings. *How could he? How could my mother not have stopped him? How could anyone do this to someone who is not much more than a baby?* We feel disbelief alternating with outrage. We feel shame for having been used in the ways that we were. We feel robbed of our innocence and the pleasures of our childhood. We are shocked, and we are very sad. We don't know what to do with the intensity of our feelings. We feel as if we'll die if we let go and fully feel them.

Long ago we learned some way to control ourselves against feeling these feelings. Whether we became amnesiac, took charge and assumed everything was our fault, or became very rigid and remote about our emotions, we were controlling what we let in. Now we cannot relax the reins without recognizing that we are as powerless over these feelings as we were over the incest. The feelings are ours, and it will be validating and helpful to own them. Our challenge is to trust that if we enter them rather than trying to resist or avoid them, we will not be swirled about with them forever. They will pass and become an integrated part of our journey.

When we are ready to let go of our old controls, we admit that we were powerless over the incest or abuse we encountered. We did not bring it on. We were not equipped to stop it. We were children with eyes of innocence, helpless. Someone wronged us deeply. We have often thought, *If only I could have stopped it . . .* but we could not have stopped it. We let go of the "if only" now and sit still with our stark powerlessness. We surrender to that feeling, whether it leaves us wanting to strangle someone or releasing great sobs of our brokenhearted anguish.

In our surrender to powerlessness, we touch ourselves with the gift of truth. We are vulnerable, and yet a new strength flows into us: the power of the inner harmony gained by our admission.

writing exercise:

I didn't make it happen. My keeping it a secret hasn't taken care of me. My worst fear of what will happen if I let go is . . .

vision:
(Example: To see my innocence and the autonomy of my body before invasion.)

action:
(Example: Each night this week I will go back over the day and inventory whatever I hid this day by keeping secrets.)

Belief in a power greater than ourselves

Do we have a belief in a power greater than ourselves that can comfort and guide us through this difficult process? Many of us do not. We may associate a power greater than ourselves with a parent who abused us or misused his or her position of authority in other ways. If we once believed in God as children, we may have lost our faith over the question, Why me? How can a God let this happen? Or because of our lack of control over destiny, we may have decided to see *our will* as the highest power and the only thing to which we dared entrust ourselves.

To heal, we need to allow ourselves to trust in a positive life force—an energy that exists within us and relates us to a larger spirit. Without developing this faith we will feel very much alone or need to be overly dependent upon other people. We are free to envision this power greater than ourselves in any way we wish. For instance, we might experience our sharing with other incest survivors as a force outside of us that is touching our spirit. We might look upon nature as our guide and consoler. We might think of our higher power as a higher self within us.

A steadying faith is not something anyone acquires overnight. We may have glimpses of it, followed by periods of doubt. We may feel its potential to soften us and be afraid of that. After all, haven't we always battled through against great odds with little or no assistance? Prayer may come out of us only when we are in dire need. Our prayer may be angry and insistent: "Show me you are there by getting me out of this fix." This will not hurt anyone, though it is more bargaining than prayer. It may lessen our resistance and fear to realize that no one is asking us to visualize a higher power who cannot tolerate our anger. Gradually, if we become more open to this force, we notice how frequently we are aware there is a place to turn for guidance that is ever-present.

In our relationship to this force, as well as in relationships to people, we can work with our feelings about trust and stretch past our old limits, facing down our fears to find that we are loved and do have a spirit guide when and where we seek it.

writing exercise:

When I was a child I believed . . . (Write for ten minutes.)

If I sum up the forces that brought me through my worse times, I see . . . (Write for another ten minutes.)

vision:
(Example: My vision is for willingness to allow within myself the notion of a power that is greater than I am who cares for me.)

action:
(Example: My action is to set aside a daily time and structure for meditation of some kind, whether it be walking, reading a meditation book, or simply staying still and concentrating on this intention.)

Returning more fully to the body

Our bodies are the homes in which our life force resides. They deserve to be treated with all the care and respect we can muster. Yet many of us who were sexually abused survived this trauma by moving out of our bodies. A woman I know describes the feeling of one eye popping out to fly up to the ceiling and look down, watching what her grandfather was doing, while the rest of her was dampened to oblivion. Some of us numbed our bodies; some of us created a separate personality in order to survive what was happening to us and keep our true personality untainted. Some of us have lived for years with the tension that comes from holding abuse memories static in our bodies. Whatever our device, it was a resourceful psyche that provided us an exit. But the price, we see now, was expensive.

As we begin our healing journey, we want and need to come back into our bodies more fully. We can choose small ways to do this, such as deciding to stay present in the dentist's chair instead of using this convenient, well-worn "out-of-body" route to avoid an uncomfortable experience. We can take baths and let ourselves savor the wholeness and goodness of our bodies. We can exercise with full attention to letting our bodies be the guide to how much is enough and not too much. As we make these forays into remaining more conscious, we often encounter grief and pain. We have the mixed blessing of experiencing new joy and at the same time recognizing what we have missed in the past.

Many of us start to reintegrate our bodies by doing body work, such as massage, chiropractic, or yoga. Holistic treatment by a sensitive practitioner or teacher can help us to become aware of which parts of our bodies we are comfortable or uncomfortable with, where we hold or block our energy, and which of our postures were developed defensively. Gradually we can experiment with opening some gates and letting old holdings go.

writing exercise:

Give yourself a talking body. *If I let my body talk, this is what it says* . . . (Record what it says for the next twenty minutes.)

vision:

(Example: I visualize my body as a container of water, as a series of lakes and streams all interconnected. If I lean from side to side or stand on my head, the water can flow freely in all directions.)

action:

(Example: I make the appointment that I have been putting off. This is the next right thing for me to do to take care of myself; for instance, a teeth cleaning or a visit to the gynecologist.)

Shame

One of the effects of coming more fully back into our bodies is that we become more aware of our shame. Most of us are awash with it. We have held the distorted idea that everything that goes wrong is somehow our fault. There was no comprehensible explanation when the abuse was happening as to why we were being abused; therefore, it would have been nearly impossible not to assume we were somehow bad or unworthy and had something to do with bringing it on.

Shame is an all-pervasive character assassinator. It squelches our very being and does not offer space for correction. Shame entraps us hellishly. But seeing ourselves as human beings who make mistakes gives us a chance to own ourselves as imperfect and to try for better the next time.

If our shame is so deep that we don't dare admit it, the first step for us will be to share it with understanding others. As we speak our shame out loud, as we hear others express theirs, we begin to compute how greatly it has poisoned our point of view and how severely we have let it punish us. When shame is met with compassion and not received as confirmation of our guilt, we can begin to see how slant a lens it has had us looking through. That awareness lets us step back far enough to see that if we can let it go, we will see ourselves as clean where we once thought we were dirty. We will remember our innocence. We will see how our shame supported a system in which the perpetrators were protected and we bore the brunt of their offense—first in its actuality, then again in carrying their shame for it.

If the method we chose to try to beat out shame was perfectionism, we can relax now, shake the burden off our shoulders, and give ourselves a chance to loosen up and make some errors. Hallelujah! Our freedom will not come from tireless effort and getting it all exactly right.

writing exercise:

Shame was like a yoke around my neck. It felt like . . .

vision:

(Example: My vision is for a clear view from a perspective that is not shame-based.)

action:

(Example: My action is to call up my landlord, knowing that I am fully entitled to and deserving of adequate heat.)

Becoming outraged

The bridge out of shame is outrage. Suddenly the obvious becomes stunningly clear to us—we have been carrying shame for the crime of the offender. We don't know what he or she has borne, but we do know our load has been excessive. In a clear flash we may see ourselves standing in a fierce stance, grounded by our knowledge, ready to throw off any wrongdoer. Our outrage can be a fueling energy, capable of making us as steely as we need to be.

In the long run, our vision of ourselves in outrage is not likely to hold steady but will ebb and flow. We will remember it, then forget it over and over again as we work our way gradually out of shame.

To *outrage* means to offend against grossly or shamelessly, while to *rage* is to act or speak with fury, to show or feel violent anger. We may be afraid to feel outraged because we're sitting on top of our rage and don't know how to express it without abusing others. Often loved ones are our closest targets, and we strike out at them with a vengeance that grows out of our past. Here we may need to use professional help and return to the scene of the crime and let out our anger directly at the perpetrator through imagined dialogue, writing letters that will not necessarily be mailed, or beating up on pillows. What's the use of expressing our rage in these ways? we ask at first. How can we be satisfied if we are not going straight to the perpetrator? But when we actually attempt such expression, we find that it helps by letting us see just how strong our feelings are. It helps us see for ourselves where our vigor has been damped down and channeled off. It lets us release the pent-up energy that has ticked away undercover for years, creating anxiety and stealing our serenity.

There is no escaping the truth that something horrific occurred in our early lives. Outrage was and is the appropriate response. Because we needed to protect a parent or other important authority figure, we were forced into a double bind. Now as we let our outrage through, we can no longer hold intact this system in which we protect that person. Piece by piece, we let that system crumble.

writing exercise:

I am suddenly swept with a great wave of indignation. "How dare you?" I say. "How dare you . . ." (Go on writing for twenty minutes.)

vision:

(Example: I visualize a fierce stance in which my outrage roots me to the ground even when I am horrified.)

action:

(Example: I will write a letter of outrage to my perpetrator. I do not need to send it, at least not now.)

Grieving

We grieve the loss of our innocence, the days of childhood that would have held more freedom had we not been huddled around our hearts, protecting, clutching against invasion, without even knowing we were doing so. Our grief may be layered with various feelings, such as deep sadness interposed with anger, or the sense we are touching our vast and long expanse of isolation. It may come to us in surprising moments, times of joy, times when we reap the benefits of our recovery. Each time we discover our new possibilities, we become more aware of what we have been missing, of the penalty we paid for our unchosen victimization.

Many of us are frightened of grief. If we did not have a protective parent holding our hand and showing us that feelings of loss were a part of living to be walked through, no wonder we are afraid. We needed someone to assure us that entering these feelings would not be the end of us, that we would emerge anew as surely as spring follows winter. Often these people meant to be our parental guides were the very ones abusing us, or they were choosing not to see our distress at whoever was our abuser.

Today we are fully capable of allowing ourselves to grieve. If we fear that we will fall into a deep pit of loss and be without consolation, then let us make an appraisal of the resources we have developed to support and protect us. Do we have a helpful therapist? A group of incest survivors with whom we share? A spiritual connection with a power (whatever way we envision that power) greater than ourselves? Close friends who listen to us? Knowing that we can call upon connections such as these to keep us in the present and give us perspective, we are free to experience our aloneness. For this stark aloneness is surely what we felt in childhood when we strongly identified with someone close to us who then violated our trust and dependence.

There is a well of life that springs from death. The dead twigs of a tree that die into the forest floor become food for the roots of that same tree as well as neighboring ones. We cannot go back and have our childhood over, but we can release our grasp at the hope of a better past and nourish ourselves by embracing our present reality, in which we are free to live fully.

writing exercise:

My losses are many-layered. They start with . . . (Describe one and keep going. One may lead to another. Describe as many as you want.)

vision:

(Example: Having losses to mourn does not mean I am lost. I visualize sitting with my losses as I might sit in a cemetery with a lost loved one.)

action:

(Example: Every day for this week I will light a candle at a certain hour and sit while it burns, honoring my losses.)

Hope

In the grief that comes with recognizing what happened to us, we often feel there is nowhere to turn for solace. We are saddened to our core and, inconsolable, we despair. Or, afraid this despair will leave us with the covers over our heads, with no motivation at all to take part in life, we resist it vigorously. We do things to keep it away, such as becoming overly busy or using drugs or alcohol to numb our feelings. When we are caught up in resistance, we do not feel hope, but when we surrender to our sadness fully, hope trickles in.

Where this hope comes from is a mystery worth contemplating. Is this a higher power letting us know there is a guiding force we can reliably turn to for comfort and guidance? Instead of clutching tightly to our problem and to the shroud of our despair, can we release it to some greater power and stop trying to do it all single-handedly? We have struggled long and hard to get things under control—our control—because a basic area we should have been in charge of (our bodies) was transgressed. So it is not surprising if we have trouble releasing our despair. But what do we have to lose by trying?

For years we have been caught up in being the victim, struggling repeatedly for survival, weighted heavily by the burden of our history and the drudgery of carrying it. Therefore, trusting to the lightness of hope is bound to make us feel vulnerable. If we are accustomed to thinking we know all about life by staying in the darkness only, we have to be willing to let go of our attempts to control in this way.

An honest assessment of our experience—then and now—is crucial to our healing. Some of us have been ruthlessly honest about knowing what happened to us, but perhaps we are less able to honestly admit we are attracted to those moments when we feel hope and would like to have more of them. Perhaps we need to admit that our fear of being vulnerable keeps us at arm's length and holds us away from embracing a hopeful attitude.

writing exercise:

I can see the darkness easily. But there is always a pinpoint of light. I see it
_____ (Describe where you see the light of hope. Go on writing
about this light.)

vision:

(Example: My vision is for faith that a higher power is guiding me.)

action:

(Example: My action is to meditate daily.)

Refusing abuse in the present

Those of us who are alcoholics or addicts know that the first and absolutely essential gesture we needed to begin our healing was to refrain from drinking or drugging one day at a time. We needed to *show up for life,* bereft as we might have been in the beginning of our recovery. As survivors of sexual abuse, we do not have a clear-cut substance to put down. Our habit is more subtle but no less pervasive and self-destructive. We are accustomed to being abused, either by another or by ourselves. Our abuse takes many forms, ranging from being in abusive relationships to listening with credence to the deriding voice in our heads—an endless record that tells us we're no good, unlovable, not worthy of praise, unlikely to experience joy.

In whatever way we are aware of tolerating abuse, we can and must make a commitment to refuse it. We have an overly developed tolerance for abuse. This does not make us saintly. It may leave us staggering around like a boxer who has taken too many punches. We may be afraid to move away from the very familiar place where we are victims struggling for survival. This is quite natural. Yet we cannot begin to heal our wounds without freeing ourselves from further injury.

We do not need to act hastily, as if everything must be changed immediately. We might do best not to even think about what abuse we took or gave to ourselves yesterday. We can concentrate on today, having faith that we will be able to see whatever potentially abusive situation is in front of us. And in this way we will make a practice of refusing abuse in the present. Perhaps this means hearing that abusive voice within us and turning it off each time it enters our awareness. Perhaps it means saying to the auto mechanic who we feel is about to exploit us for not being knowledgeable about cars, "I want to get another opinion before I say yes." Perhaps it means walking out of our home if our partner becomes physically or verbally abusive.

Whatever our gesture, however large or small, we allow ourselves to feel good about making a commitment to ourselves and carrying it through. A chorus of voices ready to punish us may grow louder than ever, but we do not let them drown out our victory. Inside us we know we have made a gesture true to our existence. It is a triumph. We do not give it away.

writing exercise:

Give some space to that self-abusive voice in you that always wants to put you down. Write a monologue from its point of view. When you've done this for ten minutes, stop and begin a dialogue by bringing out the voice that can talk back to the critical one. Be as free as you were in the voice that told you off.

vision:

(Example: My vision is for a space clean of reinjury in which my wounds can heal.)

action:

(Example: My action is to note my tendency to get bogged down in an abusive situation and to practice consciously walking away instead.)

Being attracted to the past

One of our greatest challenges is to stay in the present, to learn to be more fully in the now. We've bounced from past to future to avoid frank connection to who we are right now: a wounded person who often feels less than complete. Some of us still return over and over to an idealized past, split off from the trauma of incest. Perhaps we can remember a sense of security, of belonging, of being a part of our family, but the closeness was derived from a system of enmeshment in which we, as individuals, had no room to breathe. And we were being damaged. To come into our own we must integrate by taking in our whole experience of the past.

The parts of our past we have not encountered and made peace with always draw us back to them. They hungrily seek our energy, for we all have a deep desire for wholeness. Often we find ourselves in present life coupled with someone who provokes old injuries. He or she sparks in us a reaction which is far deeper than the one that seems appropriate to the situation. The reaction is so charged because our unresolved past is elicited. There is no sense in putting it off. We may as well trust that this is the time to deal with it. If we are not equipped to do so, then our job is to acquire the tools we need to do this dismantling.

The past attracts us not just to beleaguer us but to show us where we are caught, held up in our journey.

We can go back and open ourselves to the experience of our inner child, allowing his or her pain to penetrate through to us. We can write letters to our perpetrator, starting with some we will not mail, to give voice to what it was like for us when we were hurt. We can honor those experiences of the child within us and cease minimizing or trivializing them, allowing ourselves to know how much these experiences shape us.

writing exercise:

The part of my past that is eating away at me right now is . . . (Write for twenty minutes about this.)

vision:

action:

Creating boundaries

In childhood we are dependent upon our parents and other authority figures, yet we have a fledgling sense of independence, a small notion of how we are separate from others. We develop this sense of self by having boundaries that contain us and help us see this is me, that is you. The most obvious and concrete is our skin, which defines the limits of our bodies.

In the experience of incest our bodies were invaded. Some of us had offenders who thought we were too small to have any sense of what was going on. Growing up we may not have been permitted privacy, to close our bedroom door, to have the bathroom to ourselves. Our sense of self could hardly grow independent without sufficient room.

As we begin to heal we see that we are very young in this arena of knowing our boundaries, creating ourselves within them, and holding off the unwanted trespasses of others. Perhaps our solution has been to withdraw from interaction, especially if it is intimate. But this deprived us of close human relationships, one whole aspect of wealth in life. Or perhaps we went the opposite way, forming enmeshed bonds with another, creating the illusion we were close when actually we were so merged we couldn't distinguish ourselves from the other. This solution too deprives us.

We can begin creating boundaries according to our needs and desires. We want to make a safe space for our growth within these borders. We might think of it as planting a garden. First we need to decide how large to make it. How much is enough for us? Do we need a large space or a medium or small one? Do we need a fence to protect our bounty or will a simple border of smelly onions keep intruders out? We must keep in mind our nature. These boundaries are for us alone. There is no rule book to tell us which ones to erect. But intuitively we can tap our knowledge. Even if we erect the wrong boundaries at first, we will learn about ourselves, and no one says we can't alter our earlier decisions.

Following are some examples of boundaries we might create: I need a separate space all my own in my home where I am free to close the door; I won't tell my whole story at once when I meet someone new; I won't have sex unless I feel like it.

writing exercise:

My self needs a garden in which to grow. The boundaries I want to create to form it are . . . (Write for twenty minutes describing the garden you need, how you will make it, and how you will grow in it.)

vision:

action:

But who am I?

Our identity has been confused with that of others and with the "shoulds" that go with our class status, our race, our gender, and our sexual preference. When we first begin to create boundaries for ourselves, sometimes we don't know who we are forming them around. Our sense of who we are is weak. We don't know what we want. Why?

The old ideas of who we are all come into question. Did we really enjoy being the comedian, or was that a role we played because of our desperate need for attention? Were we loners because we were gratified by the solitude that gave us, or was that simply the only way for us to feel safe?

At this juncture we may feel very young, for it is time to take faltering steps as a toddler does, groping and exploring. We need to try on ideas of who we are, as we would experiment with clothes in a dressing room, recognizing that no, this doesn't quite fit; yes, this one does and it feels good. We need to allow plenty of space for our "I don't know." For truly we don't know. We can choose to see this as a place of adventure or as a place of panic. Chances are that the panic is the result of our fear that we will find nothing, or we will discover we are not enough, or that the "not-enoughness" we've felt all along will be exposed.

But even when we feel as if we were erecting boundaries around a vacuum, if we hold to the notion we are creating our space, soon we will experience inklings of who would like to grow there. This person might be the child within us wanting the playfulness that was lost in our trauma. Or we might discover our irate adult wanting to take up his or her power. Not an abusive power over someone else, but the ability to be whole and enter the world more fully. There is room for as many ideas of our self as we are ready to explore here.

writing exercise:

Who am I? I am _____. I am _____. I am _____. I am not _____. *I am not* _____. (Write for twenty minutes, adding to these lists of I am's and I am not's, or elaborating on one or more of them.)

vision:

action:

Identifying what you don't want

We can often more easily identify what we don't want than what we do want. There is nothing wrong with starting here. A "no" becomes a boundary. "I don't want to go on working in a field I do not like." "I'm not sure what I'd like to find in a partner, but I don't want another relationship with an active alcoholic or drug addict." "I don't want any more abuse in my life." "I don't want to be in the closet as a gay person."

If I've been living as a victim, I've had a large dose of self-pity to contend with. There may be a whining voice in my head that makes childish demands—gimme, gimme, gimme—and assures me I might as well not want because I won't be able to have what I want anyway. This is a voice of negativity. I need to distinguish it from the positive experience of defining myself through identifying what I don't want.

How does it feel to say, "I don't want any more abuse in my life?" Does it raise the specter of a vacuum, giving me a lost feeling? Who will I be without it? What will replace it? Does it offer a picture of a peaceful landscape stretching into a future? Does it feel like pulling up anchor, making motion inevitable?

As we learn to say no we commit to creating room for new experiences in life. We are saying we are worth better. Our nature is worth exploring. Though we fear we will find ourselves empty, we are willing to walk with our fear of that. The place where we have lived within our victim status no longer suits us.

When we say, "I don't want . . ." we close doors behind us. We exercise trust in the notion that, in time, new doors will open because we are willing to close the old ones.

writing exercise:

These are the places where I want to say no. I don't want . . . (Make a list of things you want to say no to. Choose one or two that you wish to elaborate on and keep writing about them for twenty minutes.)

vision:

action:

Standing up for your no

No sooner have I determined which things I don't want than I will be given the challenge of standing up for my no. I am an interrelated being. It is unrealistic to think my no-saying will be exempt from having an impact on others. Perhaps I've decided I need a period of healing without the stresses I've experienced in being sexual, but I have a partner who does not have a corresponding desire for this respite at all. Perhaps I've discovered I've put my energy into caretaking when what I've needed is to be "care-taken" more myself. But to put some limits on my caretaking of others will cause a shift in my relationships that will require a period of adjustment. It would be simple if everyone would joyously fall in behind my no, but is it realistic to expect this? Of course not.

My sense of self is fragile. I do not like having to stand fast and hold to my no against resistance. I fear I will give in and end up having low self-esteem because I have abandoned my need. I fear others will "get me" for not putting their needs ahead of mine. Sometimes my fear is so great it turns to panic—a feeling that I will be annihilated for standing up for me first. Many of these fears come from the incest, when I was made to take care of someone else's needs rather than my own.

Something does die when we stand up for ourselves—an old way of being, which allowed us to be taken for granted. The new self, who is left standing, feels awkward, alone, and vulnerable. We have little experience with this new one, so of course we feel young, and yet it is important that we stand fast when our need conflicts with someone else's. If we are not up to this alone, we can look to the resources we have developed to help us. We can tap the supportive strength of other survivors, who affirm we are worthy of our no-saying, and who tell us of experiences that frightened them but ultimately validated them and brought them into a new season.

If, after we have stood up for our no, we are plagued by inner voices echoing the original fears, we recognize these reverberations as part of the process and refrain from using them to convince ourselves that our path is in error. Gradually, without reinforcement, they weaken and die away.

writing exercise:

I remember a time I stood up for myself and said no. (Start with a memory of saying no and continue writing for twenty minutes about that incident or others it reminds you of.)

vision:

action:

Sharing your unformed self

For change to occur in us, we must be willing to enter the wilderness of the unknown and to wander in unfamiliar territory, directionless and often in darkness. We must be willing to release the righteous victim's role. That *was* who we were. That is not who we are now.

We dread the feeling of "lostness" that goes along with being in the wilderness of our unknown self. Many of us were children forced early into adult roles. We had to know how to take care of things. We tried to parent our parents so that they could grow up and help us. We don't like to be the newcomer, the student, or the patient; we are more comfortable being the old-timer, the teacher, or the doctor.

But it is time to take our turn at being unformed, unsure, not confident. We deserve to be able to let ourselves fall into fragments and feel fragmented awhile. We do not need to keep every little thing under control. In fact, we find ourselves only by allowing some falling apart to happen.

One way to begin re-forming ourselves is to share with others even when we feel lost and inarticulate. Perhaps this is our greatest challenge, for how can we share a self we know so little about? How can we overcome the pride of the person we once were who had words to explain everything away? How can we risk sharing when we are at our most vulnerable?

It is important to share with people who can understand and empathize with what we are going through. Sometimes we have no words but can only share tears. Yet it heals us to stay with what we need and not censor ourselves as we did all our lives to protect someone else. We honor that fledgling self and allow it expression.

Painful and frightening as it may be to do this, we find ourselves rewarded with a new confirmation of who we are. We have taken a step toward finding our way.

writing exercise:

I fall apart to rearrange. Some parts of me I don't even recognize, but this is what they look like . . . (Describe them. Go on writing for twenty minutes.)

vision:

action:

Allowing yourself to be

We have each been given an existence, a time and place on this planet. We are meant to be here.

As survivors of childhood sexual abuse, we may have difficulty accepting this entitlement to life. Someone invaded us and gave us a contrary message—that our *being* was not enough to protect us. We were shattered or flattened by the intrusion.

To compensate, many of us became obsessive doers. I will become the best this or that. I will prove myself worthy through straight A's or by being the most diligent worker. I will keep going from dawn to dusk and drop with exhaustion into sleep at the end of the day. In the meantime we discover this compulsive busyness keeps us from our feelings as well, an extra compensation.

Even if we take care of our physical being as part of our doings, because, for instance, exercise and going to the dentist faithfully ended up on our list of proper things to do, what of our soul? When did it get nurtured? Or was it squeezed out and deadened by our constant doing? And didn't that leave us empty?

Allowing ourselves simply to exist may be terrifying if we have spent years preoccupied with justifying our existence by doing. We need to start with small doses, such as setting aside ten minutes a day for "being" time, waking up and staying in bed long enough to ruminate over our dreams or being outside in a quiet, undirected way with nature.

At first it may feel as if nothing is happening. After all, we are used to action, to being the actor. We do not feel safe being the receiver. Weren't we once abused when we were in the passive mode? When will our ten minutes be up? How can it take so long? Here we can focus on breathing and the simple dignity we get from it, from life energy going in and out of us. We can concentrate on staying present in the moment and in the exact location where we are now. We can hear the sounds around us. We can feel the sensations of our bodies. We can let all that exists around us *be*, without judgment.

writing exercise:

When I allow myself to be, I experience . . . (Go on writing for twenty minutes about what this is like for you.)

vision:

action:

Identifying what you do want

If, as a child, my wants were not respected, or I was made to pay for them, I had good reason to stop letting them through. I may have done this so well that I am no longer able to identify them even to myself. And now it may feel dangerous to embark on the mission of trying to know them. I feel safer when I say, "I don't know what I want." But I do not feel empowered.

We start by making some distinctions. For instance, *knowing* what we want does not necessarily mean *getting* what we want. But it is a first step in making that possible. Living without knowing what we want has left us in a state of limbo, deprived of direction. Even though this made it possible to live without the anxiety that comes if we treat ourselves as fully entitled people, it leaves us undernourished.

As we begin to identify what we want, our lives may seem more painful and frustrating than before, because we may not be ready to have these things we want. For instance, we might want a fully committed relationship with mutual support and connection, yet the child within us might need more mothering before we can give unconditionally to another. We might want meaningful work, but realize to have it, we need to gain the necessary education to enter that work sphere.

It is painful to see how the effects of the incest have limited us in the past. And even though we now recognize this was through no fault of our own, our impulses will still not be gratified immediately. We must remember we are young in our recovery. When we are stymied and hear the "give up" voice, we can bring forth our adult self to reassure our inner child that we know the steps to be taken, one at a time. We don't need to be defeated even when something presents itself as difficult.

Identifying what we do want is gratifying in and of itself, regardless of the distance we have to go to attain our goals and fulfill our desires. It is important to validate and celebrate ourselves for having the strength to make choices and to listen to our inner direction.

Make a list of one hundred *I want*s. Don't be surprised if it is difficult to come up with the first dozen. Try to think of both the broad things *(I want meaningful work)* and the smaller, daily desires *(I want to be able to get a massage when I'm stressed out)*. Let yourself go back and add to this list as you move forward in this book. Write for twenty minutes.

vision:

action:

Revictimization

We have gone through a lot to move away from situations and attitudes that victimized us. We have had glimpses of a new freedom, of a full harvest within us. We have felt our shame, refused abuse in the present, and worked to integrate painful truths of our past with our present. How, then, is it possible that we find ourselves sometimes in situations of revictimization, or, if not actually experiencing them, surrounded by those same attitudes speaking as voices within us?

Vigilant as we might be, the familiarity of the old way draws us unwittingly. Also, it is quite natural to become less vigilant as we grow in confidence and gain further distance from past abuse. We relax into complacency or soar with enthusiasm, and perhaps our enthusiasm even crosses over the line into grandiosity. We are fine now. We've caught on. We'll never be exploited or misused again. And then suddenly we discover we are there. We've unknowingly given over our power to another or to that beating-up voice inside.

To recognize this feels dreadful; it makes us wonder if our movement toward wellness was only illusory. Are we stamped in this mold for life? Are we stuck in this karma? If we act for ourselves once will we be given a taste of freedom, only to know more bitterly what we are missing when we are back in the mud again?

Of course these are our feelings, not our limitations. If we have stood up for ourselves once, we can do it again and again. But why do we have to do it so often? we complain. Why are we presented with so many opportunities? How can we handle the discouragement of being set back on our fannies when we had thought we were fully on our feet?

Our growing maturity can comprehend all of this. For it is a childish notion that once established, our boundaries will never be transgressed again, or that we will not have to work to hold them in place or to adjust them. Life is more dynamic than this, and it is, after all, life that we are interested in living. We shall have to stand for ourselves, repeatedly, for the rest of our lives. As we practice doing this, we come to greater ease. The act itself seems less demanding of our resources. Eventually it may float over entirely into the positive realm—becoming only another chance to demonstrate our worthiness.

writing exercise:

Today the place in my life where I still feel like a victim is . . . (Write for twenty minutes.)

vision:

action:

Addiction

Many of us who are abuse survivors fell prey to addictions. We were split off from ourselves and felt our lack of freedom. When we discovered the altered state of consciousness we could get from alcohol or drugs, overeating sugar, or being in a swoon over sex, we were elated and experienced the relief of a way out. At last, we said, I can be me. I can laugh. I can play. I can allow myself freely to want things. I can be ambitious.

We felt as if we were being empowered by the fuel of our chosen substances and, in the beginning, perhaps we were. Some of us might not have survived without the respite they gave us. However, as our addictions progressed, as is their nature, they became yet another robber of our freedom. They came to demand primary attention, leaving us scrambling to satisfy them and often hiding this fact from ourselves and others.

We might feel that we cannot bear to withstand the pain of looking at our incest without the numbness provided by our addictions. However, the experience of others tells us that people who have not addressed their addictions do not have a solid foundation for healing from abuse. We must first put down our addictive substance, find the needed support for that, and then concentrate our attention on building some time in abstinence. We learn through this process how to use our feelings as guides and helpers rather than seeing them as monsters we need to escape from. If we find ourselves ending up repeatedly in situations of revictimization, it is a good time to take an inventory and see if we have failed to address some addiction. If we have, it will stunt our growth. Recovery from sexual abuse requires us to develop our adult self. Then our adult self must create a safe environment where our inner child will thrive. Addictions have the opposite effect. They keep us immature.

writing exercise:

The addictions I've taken care of include . . . The ones I've not yet been willing or able to address include . . . What felt good in the beginning when I used _____ was . . . (Describe this for five minutes.)

How I've grown since I've stopped using . . . (Describe this for ten minutes.)

vision:

action:

Up-against-the-wall pain

We've worked to expose the influence of the incest on us, and as a result have been deeply saddened and have begun to grieve the loss of our innocence in childhood. We've worked to take care of our addictions, and this has left us less buffered against our pain than before. We are face-to-face with our incest—the horror of it, the recognition in our core of how close it came to killing us, how badly it hurt us.

The pain at this clear-eyed look may feel as if it sends us up against the wall. There is no relief for it. It is too late to go back under the covers of denial. Besides, we have had a taste of the new and exciting places where our recovery might lead us. And we do not want to revert to a less truthful existence.

This deep pain is the pain we repressed during the incest, through whatever defenses we put up. Perhaps we stood off to the side, watching ourselves but feeling little. Perhaps we gritted our teeth and rolled ourselves up into a ball of indignation, yet didn't feel the hurt getting through to us.

Now it gets through to us and seems to be victimizing us all the more. But it is not victimizing us. We are choosing to go through this process to reclaim ourselves. We are facing a pain our psyche found a way to keep dormant until now because we were not ready for it. It is a birth pain. We will be born of it. And hard as this pain may be, we can remind ourselves that the actual incest is in the past and will stay there. We need never go through that experience again. We are adults now. We are not powerless children. If a former abuser still treats us as if she or he had power over us, we are free to walk away.

When we touch this pain, even embrace it, we touch a part of us that has long been hidden away from even our own view. We become more capable of being with the pain of another person without the sense that we have to "fix" it. To share our pain will reduce it and make it more bearable. It will also let us know that this hidden aspect of us can be shown and, when shared in the right places, it elicits compassion instead of terror.

writing exercise:

When I was a child, I put up an invisible shield against my pain. I lift it off now. This is what I find . . . (Write for twenty minutes, beginning with a description of what you find.)

vision:

action:

Inventory of what you are protecting

We each develop a system for getting by. We hunger for an equilibrium that lends us stability. Chances are, the system we know like an old shoe contains some elements that match up with our inner feelings of unworthiness, or worse—a sense that to have anything good, we must also be punished. Perhaps as a child we were abused by the parent from whom we most desperately sought love and attention. Our seeking was not aberrant but normal. *Their* sexualizing the relationship was inappropriate, yet *we* were punished by having our trust violated and suffering the devastating feelings that resulted.

Before we can let go of anything, we must inventory what we are protecting. Are we protecting the abuser from having to face his or her own actions? Are we protecting ourselves from seeing the ways we have been split? Are we holding off our rage? Are we ducking success so we will not have to encounter our fear of visibility? Are we trying to hold together some semblance of family threads so that we can ward off the potential isolation we fear?

To recognize what we are protecting does not mean we have to give it up all at once. It does mean we will be setting ourselves in motion. Each time we leave behind something we have been protecting, we encounter our vulnerability, as if we had taken off a piece of clothing that left more of our skin exposed. We exercise the patience to feel our way to a new equilibrium.

How do we stop protecting others and begin protecting ourselves? Some of us confront the abuser, either about the past or by addressing that person's behavior and attitude toward us in the present. We say, "You can no longer have this relationship with me. I am not available for it." For instance, if your mother always snoops around your house when she comes to visit, you say, "No snooping. If there's anything you want to know about me, ask. I'll try to answer your question." If your father always kisses you on the mouth, you say, "I'm uncomfortable with your greetings. Please kiss me on the cheek or not at all." Each time we do this, we get a little better at it.

writing exercise:

Make a list of the things your system is protecting. Choose the one that reverberates the most for you and go on writing about it for the remainder of the twenty minutes. For example, *I always covered for my mother when she was acting crazy.* I would write about how I did that, what my strategy was, what I got out of it, and what it feels like to imagine not doing it.

vision:

action:

Integrating anger

As we focus on protecting ourselves instead of protecting the perpetrator, anger is likely to be let loose. We may be out of control with it and dump on family members, friends, lovers, or ourselves. Matter may seem to jump around, refusing to cooperate with us. We cannot find our car keys; we lock ourselves out of the house; we break a glass, then step on the shards and cut our foot. We are irritable with our pets, who want only to curl up with us.

No one is exempt from anger. It can warn us of the need to become protective. It can provide us with the distance we need for clarity when we have moved in too close to a person or situation to distinguish our separateness. It was an appropriate response to the sexual abuse we received, but most of us were forced to suppress it. We were threatened or punished overtly if we expressed it. So we learned to muffle ourselves, turn our anger inward, or let it slowly but constantly spill over like boiling water dripping down the sides of a pot.

What does it mean to *integrate anger?* First, to allow ourselves recognition that we have it. Then, to notice our many circuitous ways of expressing it and see how we hurt not only others by doing this, but also—and perhaps primarily—ourselves. We might try keeping an anger journal and record our anger whenever we feel a surge of it before rushing to spill it over onto someone. We may discover the layer of feeling—often fear—that resides beneath the anger. We may discover more clearly how charged we are when threatened, and try to distinguish which things have the power to threaten us.

We take back the anger that was provoked by the abuse, then robbed from us. We begin to trust that we alone know best what is in us. It may take us time and practice to feel at all comfortable with this fiery feeling that is our anger, yet we appreciate the wholeness we have when we are armed with our full complement of feelings.

writing exercise:

Anger inside me feels like . . . (Attempt to describe or draw your anger. Is it animalistic? Shadowy? Heated? Write or draw for ten minutes.)

These are the things that make me angry. (Make a list.)

These are the things that threaten me. (Make a list.)

vision:

action:

Letting go

Sometimes it seems as if nothing is going my way. I am convinced I know what I want, and yet I cannot make it happen. The apple is too high up in the tree. I cannot reach it. I shake the branch, but it does not fall. Rather than walking away and placing my attention elsewhere, I become obsessed, and my frustration only increases. I walk into a long and dark tunnel until I reach a pitch of pain that feels unbearable. It seems as if there is no place to turn to find light. How do I go on?

We eventually learn to let go without having to go so far into our darkness, but this takes practice. Often in the beginning, the notion of letting go comes only when we feel helpless against our deepest pain. Sometimes that notion comes because we have placed ourselves in an environment where someone is likely to drop a suggestion on us, such as "Let go and let God." Or, "Why don't you allow yourself an extra session with your therapist?" And in our desperation, we are finally ready to stop saying, "Yes, but . . ." and instead say, "Why not? What do I have to lose by trying?"

We may feel as if we are on a precipice, about to fly off a cliff. How can we step when forward motion will take us into the unknown? We don't know. We don't need to know. What we need is a morsel of faith that we will not die if we take the risk of trying. The trying is not the effort itself but the willingness to stop the effort and become open to receiving help.

We quiet ourselves. Some of us assume a meditative position to manifest our humility, our openness to receiving. As we let go, we feel our burdens lifting. We do not have to carry our load alone. We realize a higher source has always been there, awaiting our openness to receive direction. We allow that power a presence within us now. We allow ourselves to trust that it is okay if we are lighter. It is okay if we cease trudging and hand our problems over. It is okay to comprehend that we do not have to be in charge.

writing exercise:

What stops me from letting go is . . . What I would like to let go of is . . . (This may be one or several problems. For twenty minutes go on describing them and what it feels like to let them go.)

vision:

action:

Living with new awareness

Once our incest is uncovered and we become aware of the ways we carried the burden of it all this time, we can no longer return to our old defenses against full-sightedness. We are alive with this new awareness. Sometimes it is exhilarating, such as when behaviors, attitudes, or feelings that have always baffled us suddenly make sense and fall into place like pieces in a puzzle. Other times it is agonizing, such as when we realize our old way of blindly trusting has hurt us and will have to be replaced, yet with what, we do not know.

To find our way anew requires risk. Babies and small children learn by trial and error. In large part so do recovering adults. Our trial and error does not have to be totally random. We can avail ourselves of the wisdom of others who have gone before us. We can develop a support system in which we talk over our decisions before making them, listening to the feedback of others and hearing our thoughts formed into words.

Still, we often feel as if we are groping in darkness. We encounter conflicting impulses in ourselves and have to choose a path without certainty. Sometimes in our explorations we get hurt. Sometimes we find great pleasure and satisfaction. We do not need to be ashamed when we encounter a "No," even if it hurts us. We have taken the risk to explore, and we have found out some of our limitations and the limitations of others.

Awareness sometimes paralyzes us by making us afraid to take a step in any direction. We do not want any more of the perilous way of the past. Yet there may be a void where we want to see a vision of new possibilities. What do we know of love that is not mired in abuse, seduction followed by betrayal, or the pain of repeated rejection? We do not like to admit we have been formed by these nonnurturing experiences, but only by seeing and accepting our truth will we be able to move forward. If our response to the unknown is avoidance, we may create a sense of safety, but at the expense of shrinking our psychic space.

To ease living with our new awareness, we can follow principles we have discovered to be helpful. For instance, we practice living one day at a time, focusing on whatever is before us in the present, restraining ourselves from being mired in the past or fantasizing the future. We quiet the voices that yak in our heads and listen more seriously to the direction our hearts give us. We envision the presence of a power greater than ourselves and seek its guidance.

writing exercise:

I am living with an altered awareness. This is what I see anew. (Describe what you see for ten minutes. When you have finished that, go on to the next exercise.)

When the fear that comes from my new awareness paralyzes me, these practices can help me keep walking. (Write for another ten minutes.)

vision:

action:

Learning to rest and play

We can ill afford to wait until we have worked through all our memories and feelings about incest before learning to rest and play. While it may seem to be a natural impulse—to get to the bottom of things and purge ourselves fully—we need to regularly examine the full picture of our lives for balance along the way. Besides, our learning to rest and play is an essential part of our healing.

Why is something that seems so positive so hard for us to do? Many of us learned that keeping busy, being on the run, kept us at a distance from our feelings—especially the painful ones we were interested in avoiding. Some of us took the ways we busied ourselves—becoming overachievers and workaholics—as self-esteem. "Look at me," we said, "I'm accomplishing things. This is living proof that I'm together." But whenever our inner feeling did not match our outer surface, we were doing ourselves a disservice. And if stopping to rest meant being barraged with this discrepancy, no wonder we were reluctant to cease our obsessive activity.

To play we need to let the child in us come forth, the child who was born playful. Yet, in our case, this is the same child who was violated by the sexual abuse. The child within us may have shut down against the risks of letting loose in playing, may believe the light release of play is for others but not for him or her, may be wary that relaxing will create greater vulnerability. Our inner child may safely come out to play only if we consciously give assurances that we are capable of protecting him or her from being harmed while playing.

Another reason it may be hard to rest and play is our fear of denial. Some of us long avoided facing our real experience of childhood. Perhaps we were good at playing: we never grew up, and this left us out of touch with reality. Today we have the ability to consciously assess what we have learned about our abuse and put it on a shelf while we rest from time to time. This is not denial.

writing exercise:

Close your eyes and visualize the child within you at a particular age. Assure that part of yourself that you, the adult, can make this a safe place to play. Play by writing or drawing anything you want to for the next twenty minutes. You might want to just write a list of silly words that come to you, or not so silly words. You might want to write them into a song or a poem. You might want to draw a picture of someone who makes you laugh. Trust that whatever comes to your mind to do is the right thing for you. Don't censor or judge it. Just let yourself enjoy it.

vision:

action:

Relating to your inner child

When we choose to uncover our incest, we may feel as if we have wound up on a treacherous road. At first there is relief in escaping the total isolation of our silence. There is catharsis in our telling. But our equilibrium is disturbed. To let in our memories more specifically is painful. We come face-to-face with our grief at not having been granted a safe and protected childhood. To own our true childhood may feel like punishment. When we have these feelings, it is time to ask ourselves what we are doing to heal our wounds rather than just exposing them.

We each seek the way to healing for ourselves—there is no formula—but in every case we need to develop a relationship of depth and trust with the child within us. The idea that we might have an interior dialogue with this child side of ourselves may at first seem silly or too indulgent for us. We may shrink at the notion, believing we must attack the problem only by clinging more vigorously to our adult side. When we do attempt to relate to this child side, we may be caught short by discovering how little trust this inner child has in us. Long abandoned, this child has found his or her own means of survival. Our inner child has felt disowned as we pushed away, trying to avoid encountering his or her feelings and experiences, which are ours. If we have tried to split off and leave him or her holding the painful baggage, chances are that he or she is angry and will respond to any invitation with reluctance. Yet we can make a beginning. We can bring to our inner child's attention the ways in which we have been making efforts all along to attend to him or her. Perhaps we have gotten sober. Perhaps we have spent a period of time showing up faithfully for therapy. Perhaps we have had children of our own and made great effort to rectify things through giving them the safety or attention we were deprived of.

We can make an inventory that includes both the ways in which we have been present for our inner child and the ways in which we have not. Then we can commit to becoming reliable in some small way we have not been before. For instance, if I always stop myself from crying with the same tone of voice, perhaps even with the same words my mother used on me, "Crying will get you nowhere," I can promise to interrupt this voice whenever I become aware of it. Instead I promise to tell my inner child, "It's okay, cry as long as you feel like it."

writing exercise:

Dear Little _____ (Insert your name here.) *I am writing to ask you how you are. Do you trust me enough to tell me? If you don't, can you tell me that? Can you tell me what you need from me for you to begin trusting me?* (Write for ten minutes, if you can, about how your inner child is, or what he or she needs to be able to trust enough to come to this point.)

(Now write for another ten minutes about what you think you can promise to offer. Be honest. Don't promise something that is still behind an obstacle. If you aren't ready to promise anything, write about your obstacles.)

vision:

action:

Taking power

Power is confusing for us, perhaps even terrifying, because our relationship with it had an unfortunate beginning. Someone in a position of power over us used and abused us. Their misuse of power was something that hurt us. We might have been tempted to retaliate by hurting someone smaller than we were. This, also, was not a good experience of power. It seemed as if power were something to be wielded, always at someone's expense, usually our own. Often we entered relationships in which we made a silent contract that said the other person could have the power to make the decisions for us if that person would take care of us. This didn't end in our being taken care of, but instead in our being revictimized. Our self-esteem ebbed lower and lower as we accumulated more and more the sense of being a doormat.

To heal we need to learn to take our power. It helps to recognize what that power is. It is not the power to abuse or take anything away from another, but the power to be in harmony with and act honestly for oneself. When we say no to something we don't want, we exert our power to establish a boundary. When someone fails to fulfill a contract with us, we respond with insistence that the job be completed. This is not being mean; this is an appropriate demand for accountability.

When we first begin to take power more directly, after long having kept our relationship to it underground by using tactics such as blaming or passive-aggressive guilt tripping, it is natural that we experience anxiety, even guilt, at putting ourselves first. These feelings let us know we are taking action; they do not need to stop us.

Through receptivity to our higher power's will for us, some of our anxiety about power is allayed. Because we recognize that to carry out our purpose, we must be willing to have power—the power that comes from knowing what we need and want and being willing and able to take the responsibility for getting it.

Taking our power is something we practice on a daily basis, often in the small details of life, though there will also be times we take giant steps forward. For instance, some of us decide to confront our abusers as an act of empowerment. Large or small, we allow our acts to add up. We grow more familiar with the rewards of being empowered. We establish a history of ourselves in a positive relationship to power.

writing exercise:

Every day of my life there is an opportunity waiting for me, in which I can take my power. Mine today is . . . (Describe an aspect of your life that feels stuck, or a place where you know you have put off taking an action for yourself.)

The way I'm going to do it is . . . (Write for the remainder of twenty minutes about what you would like to do about it, what obstacles are blocking you, and how you can tend to them.)

vision:

action:

Recognizing the journey

We take up some of our power. Voices heckle us with, "How dare you?" We speak back, "I do dare. This is my life. I hear you but I no longer let you take charge." We feel anxious about using our power, but we feel good too. We feel a spaciousness inside ourselves. And we discover we are more effective in getting our needs met and providing ourselves direction.

We may react to these expansive feelings by tilting to the opposite extreme and becoming inflated and arrogant, overly in-charge and directive. Having escaped the role of victim, we want a guarantee we will never return to it, so painful has it been to us. And the only guarantee seems to be to cling ferociously to our power. We have not yet developed the flexibility to negotiate. Eventually we bump our heads into the wall of our own single-mindedness. For what we have taken on is a process, not a one-way street out of town.

It takes humility to recognize the journey, to realize that we are making courageous steps toward a balanced life but still not exempt from making mistakes. Much of our learning comes out of trials. The results of our trials are often not what we thought we wanted them to be. A power greater than ourselves can guide us and help us go on when we feel too weary to face the next moment.

We learn to take hope and pleasure from the moment we are in now, the crossroads we have just reached, rather than driving ourselves rigorously forward, aiming for some end point, where we will be able to sit back and smile. Whatever is impeding us is our work now. We are gratified by our awareness and willingness to look at it. When we finish whatever challenge is before us, another will appear on the horizon. There is always something for us to feel satisfied with now, if we allow it into our consciousness. For instance, if we look back at all we have already discovered about ourselves in our journey through this book, we will be rewarded. We have established a good reputation for showing up for ourselves. Rather than focusing on what remains to be done, let us feel self-affirming about this.

writing exercise:

Close your eyes and visualize the flow of life like a river. See yourself flowing with it. *If I look back, I can see some "way stations" I have passed by. If I look forward, I can see some things unfolding.* (Write for twenty minutes, describing what you can see of your journey, looking at it from the moment of the present.)

vision:

action:

Sexuality

Can we go through a process of recovery from sexual abuse without examination and alteration of our feelings about sexuality? Probably not. As we come back more fully into our bodies, we will experience more vulnerability and, temporarily, we may find intimacy more difficult, even impossible. Some of us may realize we have assigned false values to being sexual; for instance, we have equated it with love, or we have felt we would not be considered lovable if we couldn't perform.

We may discover we have sexualized all relationships because we did not know better. We did not know we were acting out of having been inappropriately sexualized in our relationships with our perpetrators when we were mere children, sometimes only babies. We may have gone the opposite way and kept away from others, leaving our sexual affect flat and disinterested and remaining aloof from relationships that might have a sexual aspect to them. Either tack has deprived us of a genuine connection with our own sexuality.

Many of us choose to go through a period of celibacy as we encounter the deep offenses that were committed upon us in the name of someone's sexuality. Sexual abuse is not really about sexuality but about power: someone unable to cope with his or her own powerlessness dumping on a child. To reclaim our true sexuality, we must be able to say no to sex when we don't want it. We must respect our fragility and choose a partner who is also able to respect it. We must let our inner child know that he or she is safe, that we are acting as an adult out of the freedom to say yes.

We are entitled to a full and satisfying relationship with our sexuality. This is one of the rewards of the often arduous process of recovery. No matter who violated us or how many times our sexuality was robbed from us, it still resides in us and belongs to us—a gift of our creation. It is ours to feel as part of our fullness. It is ours to choose to share with another. We may feel very young as we re-enter our sexuality. We may move in fits and starts and easily fall off center as we acquire experiences that let us get to know ourselves better. But if we accept where we are at any given moment, we will not be far off center.

writing exercise:

Close your eyes and try to locate your sexuality as a feeling of energy in your body. Where is it centered? Does it flow? Where is it blocked? What does it feel like? Write for twenty minutes, answering these questions; then continue describing it and coming closer to it. If you can't find it at all and can't answer these questions, make it a character within you and invite it to say whatever it wants to.

vision:

action:

Friendship

As we come back into our sexuality, or even long before we are ready to do that, friendship is a good place for us to direct some attention. Many of us inappropriately sexualized all relationships in which we felt some connection to another human being. We may have felt that we had to, that unless we were seductive, no one would like us. Or that if someone liked us, he or she surely had the underlying motive of sexual desire.

It can be healing to enter friendships more clearly, trusting we have desirable qualities attractive to others that have nothing to do with being sexual. Our friendships may be based on the common interests we share or simply on the fact that we feel good when in the company of our friend. Friendships are a valid source of love—a place to both give and receive love. We can take in the nourishing affirmation of a hug for the loving gesture that it is.

As we deepen our friendships and work through our trust problems, we learn how to resolve conflicts in a less intimate environment than usually exists with a lover. Because in real life, when two people are being honest, there are times we disappoint or hurt each other. The test of a friendship is not whether this happens, but whether the parties involved are able to stay present with their feelings and walk through them to a resolution.

As we move away from the old role in which we were helplessly entrapped as a victim, we make friends with the people who affirm us. Their enthusiasm about us mirrors the positive experience we are having. Their loyalty and support through hard times contribute greatly to our development of a sense of safety and well-being. Valuable as it is to be the receiver of this care, we also have the opportunity to be present in a loving way to our friends. Even when our friendships bring our limitations out in the open, we cherish the gift of them. For all of us are meant to give to and receive from each other.

Sit still a few minutes and think back over the past week. Think of your interactions with friends. What have they meant to you? Have you been present for them? Why or why not? Now begin writing for ten minutes about what your friends have meant to you. There is no need to stay in the present. If you're drawn to write about friends in the past or in childhood, follow that impulse.

Write for another ten minutes about yourself as a friend—what you have to offer, what you give in friendship, what limitations you have discovered in yourself, and what you would like to change.

vision:

action:

Responsibility

What has been our attitude toward responsibility? Some of us pride ourselves on being super-responsible, yet we carry a resentment about having had to take on more than an appropriate share of responsibility in our childhood. Some of us shunned responsibility as part of our rebellion, a reaction to shouldering shame for the perpetrator's acts. Many of us manage to create the appearance of a responsible life on the outside, while inside we feel dominated by childish impulses; we are unable to grow up because we have not yet tended to the child within us.

Our recovery truly begins when we realize we are the ones primarily responsible for our own well-being. We are the ones who care the most, the ones who have the greatest investment. Though our childhood abuse left us feeling someone ought to make reparation to us, if we wait a lifetime for that, we may never receive what we need. We choose instead to face the idea that from now on, we are going to take responsibility for caring for ourselves. When we do not know how, we seek the help of those who can teach us.

What does it mean to be responsible? We might try experimenting with the definition—responsibility is the ability to respond. Have we been caught up in reacting rather than responding? What resources are we missing that leave us bereft of responsiveness? To respond we need to acknowledge our feelings and listen to our hearts. We need to own that we are worthy of our responses—they are valid and true expressions of our wants and needs.

To be responsible also means making the decisions that will let us lead the life we want to lead. In childhood we felt subjugated to the will of others, but we are no longer in that position. We are capable of initiating actions that will direct us toward growth and new strength. Of course we will sometimes encounter feelings of powerlessness over our passivity. But by eliciting the right support to guide us, we will receive the grace needed to find our way in this journey.

writing exercise:

Ways in which I have taken responsibility for myself include . . . (Write for ten minutes. Give yourself full credit.)

Some of my feelings about not wanting to take responsibility are . . . (Write for five minutes.)

Some of the ways I am not leading the life I would like to lead are . . . (Write for five minutes.)

vision:

action:

Goals and your purpose

As we awaken to what we have missed in our lives, we realize we have often failed to direct ourselves in a purposeful way. We have been impotent when it came to visualizing our desires, our picture of what occupation we would like to pursue, our sense of our true nature. Perhaps we have made starts in many different directions but have been unable to complete things. Perhaps we have exhibited great talent but have been unable to allow anyone to guide us in developing the discipline of a particular art form in which to express it. What does this have to do with the sexual abuse we suffered?

In the incest we were used. Our self was not respected. Rather, it was maliciously disregarded so that we could be forced into the service of another person's need. Even if we were indignant, we still picked up and internalized the message that we were not worthy of being respected. Overwhelmed by our perpetrators, we felt that to secure ourselves some love we had to be their puppets. This is likely to have occurred not only in cases of overt but also in covert emotional incest. All of this took away from the innocent exploration that is a child's right and pleasure—a seeking out of ways to express the self.

Now we can begin—despite our losses—to make contact with ourselves, to explore our desires and reach for our true selves. What are our values? What things give us pleasure and satisfaction? Do we have a sense of our purpose in being here? How are we on the road to fulfilling that purpose? If there are some areas in which we are not where we want to be, we do not need to beat ourselves up. Quite the contrary. That is an old habit. We need to set goals for how we can achieve what we want. Again, these goals will not be signposts we can take out of the ground and beat ourselves up with if we have not surpassed them ahead of our time schedule. They will be guides to hail us along the way and greet us as we reach them. They will be the markers of our journey.

Close your eyes a minute and think about your sense of purpose. When do you feel you are approximating it? When do you feel distant from it? Write about your sense of purpose for the next ten minutes. If you can't find one, write about what it might be hiding behind.

For the next ten minutes write down the goals that would provide you good orderly direction toward fulfilling any purpose you do not feel you are reaching.

vision:

action:

Body memories

Body memories are those pieces of information—or emotions—that are evoked by stimulating the place where they are stored. The stimulus might be an odor, a touch, a physical pain, a sight, or a sound. Some of us have chronic physical problems surrounding certain areas of our bodies, such as sore throats, gingivitis, neck pain, low-back pain, vaginal problems. Often in recovering from our abuse we discover that the weak areas of our bodies were areas that were violated. Some of our holdings of tension or dis-ease may actually reflect our integrity, for they refuse to let us pretend everything is okay when it is not.

Why do we have these body memories? Often the sexual abuse began long before we were old enough to consciously defend ourselves. Yet our psyche provided us with defense mechanisms for handling it. One of these was to dissociate ourselves from certain body parts. For instance, if someone fondled our breasts, we might have successfully felt those were not our breasts at that moment. We separated the rest of ourselves from them.

As we heal we become aware of the ways our bodies feel factionalized—which areas are numb, unfamiliar, always tense; which parts of ourselves we have hated and rejected. Some of us find it helpful to do some form of body work for integration, such as having massages or practicing yoga. As someone works methodically and consistently over each area of our bodies, we become aware of our differences in sensation. Perhaps we are incredibly ticklish and can hardly tolerate any touch on our buttocks. Perhaps we cry when someone rubs near the joint of our jaw. Perhaps we did not know that this muscle had not relaxed in years.

Slowly we learn to value our body memories and to approach them as sources that hold knowledge we can tap to help make sense of our lives and heal. If we have some grand picture of tackling all areas at once and coming out fully integrated, we gently put this aside and instead seek guidance for what is the next area beckoning us with a signal of readiness.

writing exercise:

Close your eyes and take a couple of moments to give yourself a mental massage, sweeping down your body from the crown of your head to your toes. Notice which areas feel tense or numb and are blocking the free flow of your energy. *The part of my body that is beckoning me now for attention is my* . . . (Write for twenty minutes about how this part feels, what it has held for you, how you have felt about it and treated it, and what you would like to change about that.)

vision:

action:

Self-sabotage

Whether or not we have ever given it a label, most of us are familiar with self-sabotage as a feature of our lives. We were doing well in the course but failed to turn in the final paper. We saw that someone was loving us, and we got scared and ran away from the very thing that we wanted. We earned good money but blew it on stuff we didn't really need when what we really wanted was to save some so we wouldn't have to live so close to the edge.

We each have our own ways of sabotaging and keeping ourselves down. Why is it so hard to stop exercising them? Do we need to remain the victim so strongly that we pull the ceiling down upon our own heads? There is comfort in the familiar. Also, it is important to us to be in control because as children being abused we were not at all in control. In self-sabotage we can be both the victim and the victimizer.

How do we stop this behavior? Many of our acts of self-sabotage are committed before we are the slightest bit aware of their nature. However, if we pay attention we may be able to sense a preliminary preparation, which is where the act may be interrupted. For instance, perhaps a negative voice begins circling around us, saying, "You can't have that; you're not worthy of it," or, "That's for others, not you." Perhaps we go into a foggy haze, in which case we can learn that it is important to talk to someone about why we are in the haze. We learn these signals as if they are road signs—Slow, Sharp Curve Ahead. We learn that we need help from outside ourselves in order to slow down and appraise the situation. We talk to other survivors or to our therapist or friends. Or we sit quietly and meditate.

Sometimes we self-sabotage just when things seem to be going smoothly. Perhaps this is a way to express our fear about whether it is okay for us to have a better life. We are bound to feel anxious as we leave behind old notions of our unworthiness. The challenge is not to be fearless, but to develop strategies for acknowledging our fears and finding out how we can allay them.

writing exercise:

I am about to approach a success I have longed to achieve in the past. It finally appears to be within my reach. The closer it comes, the more my voices talk. They say . . . (Write for ten minutes about what they say. If you can't hear them, make them up. Guess what they might say.)

(For the next ten minutes, speak back to them. Tell them what you think about what they say.)

vision:

action:

Speaking out without shame

We did not endure sexual abuse because there was something wrong with us. We endured it because someone older and more powerful violated our minds and our bodies. Even if we have walked through life for many years wearing a coat of shame, feeling too tarnished to want to be noticed, that posture and attitude did not constitute our true self. Even if that coat is as familiar as our skin, it is not our skin. Underneath it we are whole and untarnished.

After our first breaking of silence about our abuse, we may have felt our shame more acutely than ever. This still does not mean it rightly belonged to us, only that our awareness was heightened by our looking at the past. As we continue to speak out, we are less willing to accept this shame. Its familiarity is insidious, yet we intuitively know it is not right for us. It has distorted our perceptions. It has cramped us into a small space with no elbow room. It is time for us to remove this coat and give ourselves a chance to embrace our stolen innocence.

As we heal we learn to speak about our abuse without embarrassment. We communicate through our tone that we did not bring on nor "invite" the damages; they befell us. We do not need to whine from a posture of victimhood to communicate this. We only need to present the facts. We hand over the shame to the perpetrator who long ago walked away from us, shameless. We derive peace and spaciousness from doing this.

There are other benefits as well. We are able to notice and intercept sexual abuse if we become aware that it is happening or threatening to happen to children we know, possibly even our own. We become a source of inspiration to others who are still mired in shame. They see by our example that they are behaving as if the wrong party had been convicted.

writing exercise:

With my imagination I climb to the top of a mountain from which I can look down upon the earth in all directions. I am on granite with a 360-degree view. I shout out to the whole world about my incest. This is what I say . . . (Write for twenty minutes.)

vision:

action:

Consoling your inner child

The child within us may need attention, especially after we have stood up without shame to speak out about incest. She or he may be frightened by our increasing boldness and fear we are forgetting the danger. How can we learn to console this part of us?

Some of us discover gifts that are consoling to our child—stuffed animals, real pets, an ice cream cone. Sometimes just by hugging our teddy bear we reassure that child within that we are mindful of his or her feelings. Many of us learn ways to have a dialogue with this child. In a quiet meditative state we bring out the child to sit on our lap. We ask the child about his or her needs. We go back with the child to scenes of our childhood. We see how it truly was. We see how we were injured, then left alone, isolated with our pain and rage. We did our best to accommodate these feelings so we could survive. Often we accomplished this, at least in part, by minimizing or trivializing our experiences. As we go back, we stay with how things really were. We support rather than invalidate or question the integrity of our child.

Having gotten a true picture of what we experienced as a child, we talk to our young self from the perspective of our adult self. We tell her or him that we are present now, that this is not going to happen again, because we are strong enough to give protection. We tell our child that we are sorry these things happened to us, and that we hate the act of the perpetrator. We tell our child that we know we were innocent, and that we love her or him and are sorry for the time we pushed away from our child self rather than embracing him or her.

We give our inner child a big hug and bring her or him back inside us. Having consoled our child, we feel whole. We experience greater integration and the power that comes from that—the power of a sense of unification within us.

writing exercise:

Dear Little _____ (Insert your name.) *I understand that what happened to you has made you feel inconsolable; still I would like to console you. Can you help me know how to do that?* (Write for twenty minutes a list of possible ways to console the child within you. Ask him or her to say yes or no after you've written each suggestion and write these answers down next to each suggestion.)

vision:

action:

Learning to protect yourself

If we were not overtly threatened by our perpetrator, it was at least implied that we should cover for him or her—by keeping silent, by pretending we were voluntary participants when we were not, by carrying the shame for this person's shameful acts. Meanwhile, who protected us? Nobody. Perhaps the enraged child within has protected us by communicating to others, *Watch out! Stay away!* thus guaranteeing distance.

Many of us have strong feelings of neglect because a parent failed to notice what was going on while we were being abused. Or when we tried to tell him or her, our parent refused to believe us. Many people who've been abused and have not dealt consciously with it are not able to protect their children against abuse. If they admitted it was really happening, they would be forced to face their own painful history. This compounds the message to us: you do not deserve protection.

How can we learn to protect ourselves now? How can we come to believe—going against the grain of that earlier message—that we deserve it?

We begin by creating a safe space for ourselves with our boundaries. We open our gates to allow in people who treat us with care and respect. We gradually open up to our feelings and learn to distinguish them one from another—disappointment, sadness, anger. Jealousy, envy, joy. We learn that they are passing states, bound into layers of the past, but also that they are often signals to awaken us to a potential threat. When we stuffed them, we lost some of our natural armor. As we get that natural armor back, we learn to use it to shield us. We hold up this shield when someone comes at us with a weapon—perhaps his or her displaced aggression. This shield is not a wall. It can go up and come down as needed, unlike a wall, which would protect against invasion but leave us in deep isolation. We learn to protect ourselves in ways that allow us to be open to the flow of life.

When we fall down in our job of protecting ourselves, we do not use this as cause for self-punishment. We simply get up and begin again, recognizing we are doing as well as we can. When we succeed, we feel the healing effects of self-protection. More participation in life becomes possible. We move back from the edge of threatened survival and become freer to focus on improving the quality of our existence.

writing exercise:

In the past, my wall was made of . . . (Write for ten minutes about the characteristic aspects of yourself that you used to protect yourself against the risk of invasion, both in childhood and later. Then write for ten minutes about how you protect yourself now. For instance, are your feelings protective, or do you still often need to be protected against feeling them? Have you developed certain outer rules or disciplines to protect yourself?)

vision:

action:

Fear

What does fear have to offer us? Why would we want to own it? Doesn't it either keep us hiding out, slinking along sneakily toward some purpose, or running away to avoid things?

Fear too is an essential part of our emotional nature. It informs us of impending threat. When we run roughshod over our timing, it scares us into slowing down. It tells us when we are nearing our limitations. It reminds us we are fallible humans.

Sometimes it stops us and seems to have the power to paralyze us from taking action. It may flash us back to the past, to a time when we were under someone else's control. We want only to throw it off our backs, to disown it, to say, "Get away, I don't want you with me now. You are in my way." But we must trust that it has arisen for a purpose. Perhaps a situation in our lives today too closely resembles, even repeats, a memory of our victimization in the past. Perhaps we have embarked on a project we are not properly prepared for. Being stopped in our tracks by fear may be the only way we would be willing to let this into our awareness.

It is important to our healing to pay attention to our fear and its causes. If we built fortification around it to keep it from showing—because our survival depended upon our appearing fearless—we now need to reveal ourselves so our outer surface more truly matches our inner feeling. But it may be difficult even to recognize fear in ourselves. We may feel fury. We may feel shyness—"Oh no, not me, I'm not up for that"—when an opportunity that challenges our balance comes along. When we quiet ourselves and seek the deeper sense of what is going on within us, we may hear a small voice say, "I can't. I'm afraid."

Once we recognize our fear, it does not hold the same energy to halt us or send us spinning obsessively in circles. It can provide a note of caution and help us to treat ourselves with care.

writing exercise:

Dear Fear, what would you like to tell me you are afraid of and why? (Write for twenty minutes about your fears, where they arise from, and how they occur in your life today. Write also about how they help you.)

vision:

action:

Confrontation

When the time is right, we may find it healing to confront our perpetrator in a way that suits our feelings and our situation. This might mean making contact with the spirit of someone who is dead. Or we might build new boundaries in our current relationship with a perpetrator; for instance, we might tell a parent, "While I am working to heal from my childhood sexual abuse in which you played a part, I need to have no contact with you. It may take a year or two. I will decide if and when it is okay to be in touch again." We might request that a perpetrator commit to attending a series of therapy appointments with us. We might write a letter that we do not mail. We might revise that letter into one that we do mail.

No matter what our choice, our action shows that we have acknowledged the harm done to us, and that we have the willingness to stand up and say we will not take it. We do not confront for the purpose of getting our perpetrator to fall prostrate at our feet, grandly apologizing and begging for our forgiveness. We know this rarely happens. More often our confrontations meet with resistance, denial, or downright hostile responses. That is why we hold back from confronting until we are ready to do it simply as an act of assertion for ourselves.

The triumph comes from our standing up for ourselves, from handing over the misplaced shame to its proper holder, from the lightness we gain in this redistribution of our burdens, from the love we give ourselves in taking the action.

As we mail the letter or make the appointment, of course we feel angst and anxiety. We do not expect to make a confrontation without provoking our doubts and hearing our negative voices take a contrary stand. Yet we can walk forward, with the aid of our support network. We keep our eye on the open pasture of freedom we are heading for.

writing exercise:

Dear _____ (name of a perpetrator). Write a letter for the next twenty minutes, telling your perpetrator anything you feel like saying. Don't hold back. Let loose. Tell this person exactly what you know he or she did to you. Tell this person how he or she hurt you. Tell this person how you feel about that.

vision:

action:

Humility

Humility is a quality that allows us to see ourselves more clearly and honestly. It gives us a chance to be based on the earth (humus) and to see ourselves accurately as the human beings we were created to be.

Many of us cringe at the sound of the word, having not untangled humility from humiliation. Surely we have known humiliation in our sexual abuse experience. We were used. We were reduced to having a small and unworthy opinion of ourselves by someone who pressed an advantage. We were pinned down or held dangling or even held tenderly but against the child's sacred need for safety. So we rail at the notion that humility might make us small again and subject to abuse.

But humility is not smallness; it is openness. It is the perspective of truth. The ability to say, "I don't know." The capacity to be teachable. The knowledge that we do not need to be "larger" than life, "better" than human to deserve respect. We can allow our faults; we can develop our talents.

Our need to be "greater than" or "less than" has been a defense that arose out of toxic shame. A shameful act was committed upon us. The perpetrator walked away, leaving us with the shame. We absorbed the notion that we were somehow defective. To cover for this we constructed a false self, a masked self. And it is this self that is the overachiever or the dunce, the tramp or the puritan, the powermonger or the pathetic loser.

In our healing we learn to release our shame, to place it where it belonged in the first place. Glimpses of our true selves shine through like rays of light penetrating clouds. Standing in this light, we experience humility. Even while it gives us a sense of our essential goodness, it also lets us see where we have wronged others. For in fulfilling our "greater than" or "less than" notions, we have often run amuck. We have probably hurt others and ourselves in the process. But with humility we can also see our way clear to making the sort of amends that will show our progress and let us behave as humans who deserve and give respect.

writing exercise:

To seek humility, I first look at the ways I am arrogant and grandiose, and on the flip side, the ways I feel inferior and discount myself. (Write for twenty minutes, describing how you function in your various false selves and defenses and ending with who you are when you are in true relation to yourself.)

vision:

action:

Forgiveness

Forgiveness is a state of mind that gives us freedom from resentments. These resentments may be ones we have carried our whole lives against our perpetrator. It may seem as if they were and are our only line of defense, so how could we possibly do without them?

For some of us the discomfort of unveiling our incest is so hard to live with, we want to jump directly to forgiveness and try to bypass the pain of the interim process. But it will not do to use forgiveness to manipulate our journey. Forgiveness only truly comes when we are ready. It's as if we were planting a garden; we must first turn over the soil and add the right ingredients for texture and nourishment if we want our seeds to grow.

Some may shudder at the notion of forgiveness and feel it has no place in incest recovery. The abuse was too brutal and damaging even to consider forgiving. But those of us who feel this way may need to think about forgiving ourselves—for all the damages we have accrued by creating situations of revictimization, for injuries we have done to others along the way, for pleasure that was provoked in the incest experience itself for which we have felt guilty.

When we receive an intuitive message that the time is ripe for forgiveness, we can choose a way to do this that appeals to us. We might use whatever form we have developed for meditation or prayer. We might write a letter, one to be sent or not sent. For instance, it might be a letter to ourselves when we were young. We find our way to a quiet place within ourselves. We express our willingness to forgive. We encounter any lingering resistance we have. We encounter the fear that if we let go of the shield of our resentment, we will be left too vulnerable. We reassure ourselves that we are conscious of new means of protection, not harmful or poisonous to us, such as tapping the strength of our fellow survivors or receiving guidance from the higher self within us.

To forgive is not to forget. Even if we forgive our perpetrator, we do not forget the acts or damages that were done to us. We still hold people accountable for their actions. It is the weight of judgment we release.

writing exercise:

I'd like to think about forgiving _____ today. (Fill in a name or names. It could be your own or the names of others.) *But I feel _____ at the thought.* (Write for ten minutes about what you are feeling as you have these thoughts. Then write for ten minutes about how you might prepare yourself to become willing or ready to forgive those whose names you listed.)

vision:

action:

New freedom, how to stay with it

When we have forgiven ourselves and others, we enjoy a new freedom. It comes to us without effort. We feel eased of burdens we have long dragged like a broken wagon behind us. We feel spacious and more open to exploration of new territory. We see choices we may not have seen before. It's as if there were an open pasture before us, which we never saw as ours until this time. Now we are free to enter it.

But as we enter it, we are bound to feel ambivalent. We are so accustomed to being restrained by our voices that say, "You can't!" "Not you!" or to being fogged in by our depression, as clouds block the brightness of the sun. We are used to the claustrophobia of walls close around us, but not to open territory. We are used to struggling and grappling just to keep plugging along for survival, but we are not used to the freedom to make choices, make mistakes, and trust our own sense of direction.

Rather than being joyous with our freedom, we may feel insecure and frightened by its newness. As if we were in the center of a vast desert under a great radiant sky, we may feel lost, undirected. It might even seem desirable to grope our way back toward some of the constraints of victimization. We feel young and inexperienced in this territory. We are. We feel fragile and vulnerable. That, too, we are.

So how can we stay with it? We can consciously choose to remember that even if we feel young, we are grown up now and have gained a lot of knowledge in our struggle to reach this point. We can reassure the child within us that we are present as an adult. At the same time, we can look to our child to come out as an explorer and let us be willing to risk experimentation. We can sit still with our fears and wait until we feel safe enough to venture farther. This sitting still is not self-defeating procrastination; it is like bread dough set aside to rise with yeast and time.

Slowly we build our tolerance for enduring freedom and let in the joy of encountering it. Slowly we become confident that this is the life that was meant for us and not just for others.

Draw a fence down the center of the page. On the left side of your fence, write about the elements that hold you back. On the right side, describe what you see for yourself in the open pasture of new freedom. Write for twenty minutes.

vision:

action:

Loving yourself

We were born in a state of self-love and knew this feeling of warmth and harmony in our hearts before we could even walk or talk. But because we were treated neglectfully and abusively in our young years—when we most needed this self-love to be mirrored—it was difficult to hold on to. When, with loving input, it would have developed, it shrank instead.

Now we are free to go back to those early feelings of self-love that were part of our creation and build anew to expand them. We take up the challenge of learning to love ourselves, through our highs and our lows, when we are finding acceptance from others and when we are being closed out and rejected. We learn to hold ourselves consolingly when we are in pain. We learn to release the anger that we formerly misdirected inward. We learn to give ourselves the gift of healing through shedding our tears instead of holding them back.

Even if our survival skills have become impediments we would like to let go of because they have ceased to serve us, we can still love ourselves with them. In appreciation of our survival, we can be awed at how our resources brought us through, even when these resources were things like indifference, a wall of rage, a cold heart. That we used whatever we could find to protect ourselves when protection was not forthcoming from trustworthy adults is not cause to make us unlovable. We learn to embrace ourselves as humans with faults and problems.

Loving ourselves is a state of being and in that sense requires nothing. Yet it is important for us to learn to be demonstrative with this love we have. There are many small ways we can do this. We can check in daily, hourly, in the moment, and say, "This holds no matter what—I love you." We can buy ourselves flowers. We can cook a nice meal and savor eating it. We can take a walk and enjoy the outdoors— each scent, color, and form we encounter. We can choose good company when we want to be with a friend.

writing exercise:

These are the ways I have demonstrated my love for myself in the past. . . . (Write for five minutes.)

This is what I feel when I think about the idea of loving myself more fully. . . . (Write for ten minutes.)

These are the new ways I'd like to add to demonstrating my love for myself. . . . (Write for five minutes.)

vision:

action:

Letting in the love of others

The more self-loving we become, the more possible it is for us to let in the love of others. It may even come as a shock to us to see in retrospect how little we were able to let it in before. As long as we were convinced that we were unworthy, we suspected anyone who thought us lovable of being either foolhardy, deluded, or phony.

In order to survive our youth, many of us became sensitized to which conditions we had to play to to receive attention. No wonder we mistook this attention for love. We thought love came in finite quantities—it had to be competed for among siblings, or it had to be paid for with exacting dues. Others of us had sexual acts forced upon us by the very people we thought loved us—our parents or other family members. How distorting this was to our notion of love!

As we heal, it helps us overcome some of these distortions if we can open a door to the love of a power greater than ourselves. We are all part of this creation we call *life*. Love flows through us. It is not finite but regenerates by flowing. As we give it, we receive it. This love from a power greater than ourselves may come through our friends, lovers, children, trees, flowers, animals, and our fellow companions who are healing side by side with us from sexual abuse. Its sources are unlimited.

If we have the willingness to open our hearts to giving and receiving love, there will always be a place for it. We may have a rigid, predetermined view of exactly what would be the right and only place for it. If we cling to this, we limit our vision. The root of our desire to know the unknowable and thereby block out the mystery of love lies in our need to control. We have an overly large helping of this because we were unable to control the occurrence of the incest. We can take care of ourselves now. We can afford to let go of our rigidity and enjoy the mystery.

writing exercise:

In my present life, which are the sources that are providing me with love? Are there sources reaching out to me that I am not receiving? Why? What am I afraid of? Where are my predetermined views functioning to cut me off? (Write for twenty minutes about your feelings about letting in the love of others, using these questions to get you started.)

vision:

action:

Being with a partner

To create true partnership with another requires more than love. Most critically it requires mutual respect and support. We must be willing to retain our autonomy while coming close to another. We must also be willing to recognize and validate the autonomy of our partner.

Many of us grew up in families where we saw none of this modeled. We were taught to enmesh ourselves thoroughly, to be dependently bound to the others in ways that certainly did not empower us. For instance, one of us served as a scapegoat the whole family dumped upon; one of us took the role of being super-responsible but was not allowed to express feelings. Or we were taught to take others who lived with us for granted, as if they were objects of furniture in our environment, whereas the real people lived outside our house.

Furthermore, as victims of incest we received the message that we were "less than." In the relationship with our perpetrator, we were certainly not respected. On the contrary, we were stung by a high degree of disregard.

Despite this poor training we've received in the past, we can and will learn to partner if we wish to. We do not need to be resigned to isolation or to repeating these old ways in our relationships indefinitely. Respect for another's autonomy is something we can learn. So is respect for our own.

We begin by learning to listen to others. One of the gifts of joining a group of incest survivors is that listening becomes an active skill we acquire. When we enter a relationship we continue to keep other aspects of our lives vital. We do not drop our friends or lose interest in our work. If we find ourselves slipping into feelings of loss of self, we step back and keep some distance until we can rebalance ourselves in the relationship.

We must also be capable of confronting our differences with our partner rather than giving up things we want and need and that help to define us. It is normal and natural for two people who grow close to encounter some conflict. We must create a healthy environment where we can express our feelings and learn to negotiate compromises that will be mutually agreeable.

Write for ten minutes, describing the ways you were taught in your family of origin to treat others close to you who did not respect the autonomy of either yourself or the other person.

Now write for another ten minutes, describing the ways you have learned to treat yourself and others who do respect autonomy.

vision:

action:

Trust

Perhaps the greatest challenge of our healing is to learn to trust other human beings again. We trusted with ease as small children who had little sense of distinction between ourselves and others, especially our parents. Like a raft on a river, we floated into life with an assumption of trust.

All children are presented with experiences in which they lose this primary innocence and discover there are times not to trust, but many of us were abruptly and horrifyingly clipped by the incest in a severely traumatic way. One of our defenses may have been to split off and leave intact a part of us that could cling to an idealized version of our relationship to our perpetrator so we did not have to face this loss of our trust in this person. But even if this served to help us get through childhood, it left us with a legacy of trusting without a solid basis.

In our healing we first inventory and admit how shaky we are about trust. Do we tell all immediately, throwing ourselves open before doing any appropriate exploration of another person's reliability? Do we isolate and stay so wary and distant that we find out little, but feel as if we are keeping safe? Do we set up a system of testing the other person in which our bottom line is to demand perfection?

Trust is the feeling of comfort and security that comes over time as we share ourselves and receive nonjudgmental and caring responses in return. We build it on a series of repeated positive responses. We learn to look for consistency without expectating that no mistakes will be made. We learn to trust our gut feeling when there are discrepancies between someone's intentions (usually spoken) and their behaviors and actions. We have a tendency to tune in to the warnings of our gut feelings but then contradict them with our own inner talk rather than acting on them. Perhaps we do this out of the fear that we will be punished or abandoned if we follow through in acting for ourselves rather than for anyone else. But we learn too that no one hurts us more than we hurt ourselves through self-abandonment. Our first building block is to learn how to trust ourselves.

writing exercise:

A time my trust was broken was . . . (Write for ten minutes, describing an incident in which you remember a rupture of trust. Then write for another ten minutes about someone you trust now. How did you establish this trust? How has it been tested? How do you feel about it?)

vision:

action:

Humor

Humor is a step back, a perspective that allows us to view horrifying things from a slant, without being as devastated as we would be without it. For instance, in a group of incest survivors, one person described a newly emerging memory of how her grandfather had rubbed his penis against her neck when she was two, using that space between her soft little shoulder and her ear, before moving to her mouth. Later when we were talking casually, another woman said, "That way you described your grandfather doing it. That's exactly what happened to me as a two-year-old." Yet another woman said, "Me too. What is this? The generic two-year-old experience? What do they do, go to perpetrator school and get instructed? 'Now take a two-year-old and . . .'" There was a great burst of healing laughter as we pictured a perpetrator's school being exposed by its victims.

We have had devastating experiences and been profoundly influenced by them, *but we are not those experiences,* and humor helps us to see from our wholeness. It offers lightness when the weight of our burden might otherwise sink us. It offers the chance for a wry turn when we are plunging straight down into what seems to be an abyss. Perhaps it has saved us more often than any other feature of the human condition, whether we have recognized it or not.

Some of us have been humorless and joyless, trudging through life as if to let anything through but grimness would be self-betrayal. Perhaps we have needed to do this because we are trying to get recognition for our woundedness. The first and most important person from whom to get this recognition is ourselves, but we can do that and also allow ourselves lightness and laughter without betraying anything.

If we grew up in an environment where humor was used as avoidance, or sarcasm was used as a cover for hurting people, we may need to purge our humor from its meaning in the past and consciously build a healthy relationship to it. Otherwise, we are missing one of our most leavening resources.

writing exercise:

There's nothing funny about this. Or is there? (Write for twenty minutes about an incident that amused you, or write a humorous description of a perpetrator, or draw a cartoon of one. Or if you can't think of anything you'd rather write about, write a sketch about a perpetrator school.)

vision:

action:

Sharing your knowledge

We have all grown up in a society in which a veil of silence hangs in the air when it comes to honest disclosure about incest. Most of us were exposed in school to some discussion of the function of taboos in society. Incest was at the top of the taboo list in most societies. The impression given to us was that because of this taboo, incest rarely occurs. Now when we can read statistics that reveal one in three American girls is molested by age eighteen, and one in five American boys, shouldn't we ask: Which is the true taboo in our society? Perpetrating incest or speaking out about it?

Once we have opened ourselves to and owned the sexual abuse we have been through, one of our greatest healing tools is sharing our knowledge with fellow survivors who are more newly embarking on this path. This sharing has many beneficial effects on us. It helps us recall our earliest horrification and remember how topsy-turvy our world became when we began looking at this. In the remembering, we realize we have been able to move on from that very unstable condition. We have an opportunity to validate someone who may not yet be able to fully believe him- or herself, and, in doing so, we affirm our belief in ourselves and document our progress. Our sharing of our knowledge is an example to another and begets another generation of people who will be able to share their knowledge in the future.

If we have dealt with our incest extensively but have done it alone or primarily with a therapist and have not met up with other survivors along the way, we may still need to find a place where we can pass it on before we can feel secure with our healing. Because the experience itself was extremely isolating, a vital part of our healing comes from joining the world from a place of honest disclosure about who we are. This includes our past as well as our present. Our wounds have weakened us; they have also strengthened us. Hoarding is never a source of strength. While we need to be mindful of taking good care of ourselves—and that includes sticking by the boundaries we require and not telling what we don't want to tell—when we can share our knowledge about incest, we are likely to find our generosity rewarded.

writing exercise:

Close your eyes and reflect a few minutes on how you got started on this journey. Even if you remembered your incest all along, what gave you, as Ellen Bass and Laura Davis so succinctly put it in their title "The Courage to Heal." Write for ten minutes about how the sharing of others, either in word or example, affected you. Then write for another ten minutes about what you have experienced when you have shared your knowledge and hope with others.

vision:

action:

Taking your right-sized space in the world

Because of the invasive nature of sexual abuse, we derived the impression from it that there was no place for us just to be ourselves comfortably in the world. We were objectified by being used. Our dignity was robbed. Our needs for autonomy and privacy were overridden and discounted.

How did we react to this? Often we fluctuated between being too big or too small. The "too big" stance took us toward grandiosity. We were too good to mix with others; we were too important to be a worker among workers. It was hard for us to be the student; we needed to be the authority even on subjects of which we knew little. We tried to create an impenetrable front, but always, hidden behind it, was the notion that if we were simply ourselves, we would not be enough. Sometimes we went to the other end of the spectrum, taking the position of being small, thinking, couldn't we get away with being invisible, dismissable? Couldn't we act out the message given to us by our perpetrator that said we didn't count? Couldn't we avoid the knowledge that to grow up we must ultimately become responsible for ourselves?

In humility we are related to the earth of our planet and can know ourselves as real. We are in touch with our whole being—our strengths and our resources, our limitations and errors. We know we are like other people at least as much as we are different from them. We are a human among humans. We do not need to perceive ourselves as unique or isolated. We belong as much as anyone does. We are of the people. We accept our story; it is the only one we have.

One of the gifts of our healing is that we no longer need to construct an outer presentation designed to hide us. Our masks are falling away. Not because we have become so extraordinary and fabulous, but because we have simply become able to be ourselves. We do not need to show up in some special costume or facade, because we are just fine as we are. We only need to show up and let ourselves be.

writing exercise:

This is who I am when I am right-sized. . . . (Write for twenty minutes, describing who you are when you are in a right relationship to the world. You might describe how you look in the mirror, how you look in relationship to other people, or how you are at work.)

vision:

action:

Stories of abuse survivors

These stories written in response to the first ten writing exercises are included to help you launch yourself into your own story by showing you how others responded to the suggestion of the exercises.

Remembering

Right now the uppermost memory that comes to me is when my grandfather was in the room but not really present. He stood against the wall with his arms crossed over his chest. He didn't say anything. My grandmother sat at the table with us and poured out tea from the teapot and said, "John, won't you come sit a minute?" He said no, I guess, but I don't remember his voice. He didn't seem to have one very often. He seemed like a piece of furniture. I was interested in the cookies on a plate by the teapot, and whether my grandmother would decide to read our fortunes from the tea leaves later, and keeping track of him without actually looking at him.

When I was two I believe he stood by my bed or crib side and put his penis in my mouth. I have bad gums now, which I attribute to my repugnance at this. I believe this happened because I've had visions of it, then seeing his back walk out the door with a dismissal, as if there was nothing of note that had happened. Even though I believe it, it's so hard to *really believe,* because who would do such a thing?

When he died I had not remembered this. I looked at him in his coffin and I felt very relieved and glad, and it seemed very strange and heartless of me, so I pretended to feel otherwise, but I like knowing it now. I *was* glad. I could look at him directly, and I didn't have to keep track of him anymore.

—MAUREEN

Breaking the silence

I could not tell my mother that the man in the woods put his finger under my underpants and I couldn't get away. I was afraid she would blame me. "Why did you stay there? Why didn't you immediately say, 'What do you think you're doing?' and get up and run away?" I could not tell her I was paralyzed, that this man kept his eyes on me, that he made me feel a fire that I hadn't known was there, that it wasn't that easy to move, that part of me was dying of horror and another part was coming to life.

I could not tell anyone for years and years that this happened to me. The man asked me to sit down beside him. I didn't know how to say no, so I sat down. I worried my brother would come and catch me. I worried my brother would not come and save me. I didn't ask for anything, but the man talked softly and rubbed my bare leg with his hand and my mouth kept swallowing and trying to say, "I've got to go," and opening and closing like a fish mouth.

I was eleven. I did finally say it and run, but he had already touched my most precious place and somehow took it away from me.

—MAUREEN

Cracking denial

The first time my therapist suggested that I was a victim of sexual abuse, I grew rageful and told her she didn't know what she was talking about. I reminded her that I came from a good, loving family, and that such things did not happen in families like mine. I told her in no uncertain terms that I did not wish to discuss the matter any further—though if she felt compelled to talk to me about it, she was not to use the words *incest* or *sexual abuse*. I was so angry and upset with the very idea that I could be a victim of incest that I even rearranged a book in her office to avoid having to see the word *incest* that seemed to scream out at me from its dust jacket.

It was after rearranging the book and returning to my chair in her office that I found myself chuckling over what I had just said and done, begrudgingly conceding that an alcoholic in treatment behaving as I had would certainly be labeled as in denial. This painful concession was the first step I took towards acknowledging the possibility that my therapist perhaps was right.

—RICHARD

Assessing the damages

Between the ages of five and eight I became a sexual plaything to an older male cousin who lived with my family for about three years. He was often put in the role of baby-sitter. I was a "good little girl," quiet, shy, and very obedient. I never knew that I could or should say no to someone using my body for their own pleasure. I had no one to talk to about my feelings. I felt alone and confused in the experiences of getting his attention and being used for his sexual pleasure. There were so many conflicting messages in the experiences. One had to do with authority figures. Because I always had to be the "good girl" and obey, and yet because an authority figure had been abusing me, I grew up completely distrustful of anyone who wanted anything from me and entirely resentful and rebellious against people who had a right to expect something of me (e.g., employers, traffic officers). My behavior around situations involving "authority" could be very erratic. While I could in some situations be the "model employee," in others I might be totally intolerant and manipulative to get my way. There was never a sense of balance between having my sense of self and hearing someone else's feelings or meeting their needs. The most important part of the damage was a complete sense of distrust of all people. For most of my life I felt that anyone who gave me any kind of attention, who wanted to get close to me, was simply trying to get something from me. Because I operated from this sense of anyone's motives, I thought I had to do my best to both pretend that I was okay with relating to them but at the same time be assured of keeping them out of my inner space.

—ELVIA

Recognizing powerlessness

It wasn't my fault. . . .

When I think of this topic, I realize how helpful it is for me to visualize myself as a child or an infant. How innocent I was. I can recall the guilt and fear I had around the incidents of abuse. I think most children take responsibility (sometimes with magical thinking) for the actions and motives of adults. It was most certainly true for me. I have believed it was my fault for most of what happened to me as a child. I was sexually abused by both my mother and father as well as a neighbor. Today, I am examining my beliefs about these childhood happenings and am realizing that I did not have the power to cause them. I was powerless over the adults in my life and also powerless over my own instincts. I did whatever was necessary to survive. My sexuality had been aroused early in life, and that put me on a path I would not have otherwise chosen. My instincts were altered by the powerful adults in my life. Today, I realize that I was innocent and not at fault even though it seemed otherwise at the time. It is up to me as an adult to recover and go on with my life, to release the pain, resentment, and anger that keeps the abuse alive. I have used psychotherapy, the Twelve Steps, visualization, and hypnotism to facilitate my recovery and to help me release the blame, resentment, and pain.

—MIKE

Belief in a power greater than ourselves

When I was a child, I believed . . .

Well, I'm not sure that I truly believed this, but it certainly came through my thoughts many times: I often thought that maybe we were all just thoughts in the mind of God—or maybe even His toys, or something. This would occur to me every now and again—I can't remember any specific time that I thought it. I never consciously asked, "Why me?" at the time, and I don't ever remember thinking the sort of standard question, "If there is a God, how could he let this happen to me?" Seems like I was taking the "sting" out by imagining that my life was just part of God's thoughts. Not *real. That's* what it was—I was making my own experience *not real.* "Etherializing" it all, making it into a dream. I *believed* that life would have been much better if my mother had lived. I spent a lot of day-dreamy time "knowing" that my life would be better, softer, if my stepmother wasn't around. I'm combining both writing assignments, realizing that I have often gotten through very difficult times in my life by going "dreamy," letting go of the difficult present and going into a softer, gentler state of being—fantasizing, imagining. Sometimes fantasizing someone loving me. Later in life going into a soft, meditational sort of space. Lately feeling gently nurtured by the universe.

When I went to church as a child, part of me was very aware of being proper, trying to pretend I was listening to the sermon, trying to *look* like a pious little churchgoer. Another part of me was in the dreamy place, just tuned in to the beauty of the choir music and the light coming through the windows—that was my connection with God, though at the time I couldn't have articulated it at all.

I think that the "dreamy" state means being *out* of my body. I'd like to be *in* my body—feeling its life, its pulsations—and truly know that this is also my connection to God.

—Diane

Returning more fully to the body

Waaaaaaaaaaaaaaaahhh! Pain in my heartpaininmyheart. Tummy grumbling, throat wanting to scream. You push up against the edges of my pain and go away, run, fly. I feel you flee—out the hole in the solar plexus, through these eyes that suddenly become vacant and staring when you stop focusing energy through them. Boo! I won't "get" you if you stay to look, feel, sense, inhabit. I cannot release myself from this painful iron grip. I need your help, your willingness. I am screaming for you to pay attention to me.

I try to give it to you through signals, obvious signs. A language of symbols we can both understand. Why do the boils on your ass erupt when hidden rage is boiling? Why do you so often have a pain in the neck, and are so often resentful of others' needs? Why are your shoulders dislocated? From the strain of supporting those who give you no support in return? These arms ache and tire. From the strain of holding them out, open, so long for love? The heart twisting into a pretzel from the effort of pretending you are more cared for than you are by Some Important Ones?

This is not a test. This is the real thing. This is your life, not a dress rehearsal. All this torture inside of me will never go away unless we work together. You need to learn respect for my ways, my strengths and weaknesses, what is unendurable stress and what is merely a fear-boundary to be gently pushed through. You and I want the same thing. Why do you hate me so?

You turn on me. You call me fat; you hate that constant kinesthetic awareness of blubberyness around your middle, *our* middle; the arms that have gone flabby too early, the cellulite creeping over your thighs. Yet you fear to let me run, dance, stretch, move that stuck energy out. You don't want to experience these sensations I give you, my "hellos." You don't let *me* run; instead you, consciousness, run away from me.

It is about bearing, and at the same time, not being overbearing. You let me reinjure myself because once you start, you have to push, have to have complete freedom from this disgusting state *now.* It's all the same thing. You're still not facing what they, and for a long time *you,* have been putting into me. Accepting poor and unreliable nourishment of every kind, leavened with a cruel impatience. Mommy and Daddy together, again. In me. In us.

You have put this un-condition there in me. I am the guardian of the secrets you have not been able to face, and also your means of being in the world at all. You love and hate me for both these things. You so often use and abuse me for your purposes, your will, forgetting to ask what *our* purposes are, what higher will might have in mind for us.

Enfold me in the love you are capable of; let the grounding I provide for you speak to you in gentleness. Embrace me as your teacher, child and friend, your partner in discovery, your ally, even your playmate. Don't turn it on and off like a faucet. You're getting better, but still you hurt, abuse, and ignore me every day. I don't want to have to scream at you.

—DANIELLE

Shame

Shame was like a yoke around my neck. It felt like the ends of the yoke were weighted down with boulders dense with the heaviest ore known to humankind. The weight of ages. The weight of all the slurs and malicious gossip heaped up in a tower of rotting garbage laced with maggots of meanness. I wore shame like a birthmark spread across my skin, like a fireworks display, ready to burst into flame with any wrong move I might make, any action that would expose who I really was—the rotten fruit, discarded after 1,002 bites. Thrown out the car window onto some lonely lot. The rats eagerly awaiting to scrape at it with their filthy claws.

Shame kept me tightly bound in its corset of correctness. No jiggling please. No unsightly bulges waiting to rupture their pus across my belly, leach down my leg, pool at my feet to the shock and disgust of all who caught sight of my disgrace.

Shame kept me a liar—prime wearer of masks that never fit, never really covered the inadequacies that formed my gross features. Masks that chafed the skin of my lies, that spun their densely matted webs over anything that was sweet or fresh about me. Nets that caught me in my rushing to escape the truth and trying to outwit and elude anyone who tried to get too close. Anyone who wanted to hold me captive in their desire to know me.

Shame kept me inventing who I should be rather than being easy with who I was.

Shame was the constant in my otherwise transient and chaotic life. Shame was the sister of my depression.

Shame fueled the fire in my sexual forays with drug addicts.

—TSURAH

Becoming outraged

I am suddenly swept with a great wave of indignation. How dare you? I say. How dare you not respond. After all you have done, after all you have left me with, how dare you not be able to say anything more than, "Kids do that to each other." How dare you call me up to ask for Eileen's number. How dare you go on as if nothing important has happened. What happened—what you did to me—changed my life. I wouldn't be calling you from the hospital if it wasn't important. Kids don't do that to each other. If you were jealous of me, that was your problem. If Mom and Dad didn't pay attention to you, that was their problem. What you did was make your problem my problem and I'm tired of it; I'm sick and tired of it. No wonder why you're so messed up. If someone did what you did, I imagine they'd be so sick inside, so sick inside of living with themselves—but that's how you felt in the first place. I wonder who you're abusing now. Besides yourself. Well, I'm sick and tired of abusing myself because you abused me. Take back your hands around my neck. Take back your teeth on my skin. Take your hands off my body. It's all yours now. All yours. Right where it belongs—on your neck, on your skin, on your body. How dare you to have made my body yours. How dare you not say you're sorry. I am. For staying quiet all this time, for so many years. No more. I've told you and I've told you it's yours.

—KENNY

Grieving

My losses are many-layered. They start with the feeling it is not quite okay that I have been born. My sister is only a year and a half old. My father is sailing a merchant ship and whenever they go through the Strait of Gibraltar, the fleet is torpedoed. Jews are being gassed by the thousands. There is a rift in civilization. It is 1943. My mother tries to nurse me only for two weeks. She says I chewed on her nipples and it was torture. I wanted too much milk. I didn't have any teeth, I point out. She never says, "I didn't have enough milk." This is a karma that I hope to recycle: that whenever I want anything, it is too much.

Other losses: My father touching rarely and almost always roughly, my mother's tension crowding under my skin. My sister saying she and her friends wanted to play with me, then changing her mind and telling me to go away. My mother making me feel like a shlump for complaining, when she might have noticed their cruelty instead. My tears meaning nothing but discomfort to her.

More losses: I couldn't flirt or subtly communicate when I liked someone and wanted to get to know them. I became tongue-tied. I became bound to my mother with some crazy loyalty. I could be fluid with someone I didn't really care about. Then they would like me and attach like a noose around my neck, while the person I wanted to be with would be walking away without knowing anything of my desire.

Innocence.

Un-self-conscious pleasure in my body.

A warm safe feeling that the future is friendly.

—MAUREEN